CATHOLIC PLANNER

2021

____

Welcome to the Catholic Planner Family! The Catholic Planner was created to help you accomplish all of your goals, stay organized, make time for yourself and your loved ones, and stay grounded in your faith throughout the year. We pray that this simple and effective tool will help you on your spiritual journey.

WHAT'S INSIDE?

Path to Sainthood: This beginning-of-the-year exercise is meant to help you reflect on the person that God is calling you to be. You will fill out each section of this chart to pinpoint your goals for 2021, while ensuring that these goals align with God's will.

Monthly Calendar: These pages give you an overview of your whole month. You will find the liturgical calendar, along with saint feast days and a saint of the month here.

There is also space to brainstorm your goals for the month. This is a great way for you to kickstart your month and move forward with focus.

Weekly Retreat: Prepare spiritually for your week here. The readings for the upcoming Sunday's mass are provided for you and a snippet of the Gospel reading is featured. We encourage you to take out your bible to read all of the passages. Below the readings you are given space to reflect on the message you read.

The next section gives you space to write down how you were in awe of God throughout the week. This allows you to always be aware of God's presence in your life and highlight what you are grateful for.

The rituals and habits section helps you to get your life into a rhythm. You can list the rituals and habits you want to develop and check off the days you accomplish each one. Good daily habits are personal activities that are important to your own well-being (i.e. drinking 8 glasses of water, exercising, practicing a passion, etc.). Catholic rituals are religious activities that express your love for Christ (i.e. attending daily mass, attending a scripture study, performing acts of charity, etc.).

The prayer list helps you to add focus and structure to your communion with God.

Weekly Calendar: These pages give you space for you to schedule your daily appointments and jot down any notes and tasks to do throughout the week.

MAKE IT YOUR OWN

There are many ways to use the Catholic Planner. Discover the best way to use the Catholic Planner that is most effective for you. Put your personality into it and add some color. Make it your own!

KEEP IN TOUCH

For more tips on how to use the Catholic Planner visit us at CatholicPlanner.com. Follow us on Facebook at Facebook.com/CatholicPlanner and on Instagram and Twitter @CatholicPlanner. Share how you've personalized your Catholic Planner and tag us!

Make this your best year ever by setting goals for yourself for 2021! The Path to Sainthood helps you to look deep into what God's purpose is for you, so that you can come up with these goals.

> "Jesus, help me to simplify my life by learning what You want me to be and becoming that person."
> - Saint Therese of Lisieux -

INSTRUCTIONS

2020 Achievements: Write down the achievements you were most proud of accomplishing last year - big or small.

God's Blessings: Reflect on the gifts that God has brought into your life. What are you most grateful for? What talents and curiosities has he given you?

Inspiration: Write down the names of people who are inspirations in your life. These can be saints, friends, family, priests, teachers, or anyone else you can think of. Also write down the qualities and traits that make these people inspirations to you.

Focus: Reflect on the categories in your life that you feel called to focus on, develop, work on, or maintain. Examples of these categories can be the Seven Virtues, the Fruit of the Spirit (Galatians 5:22-23), your family, your career, or your creativity.

2021 Goals: After filling out the previous sections you should have a better idea of what is most important to you and what God is calling you to do or be. Set goals for yourself based on the direction given to you from your answers. Don't be afraid to dream big!

> "Be who God meant you to be and you will set the world on fire."
> - Saint Catherine of Siena -

MY PATH TO SAINTHOOD

2020 ACHIEVEMENTS

GOD'S BLESSINGS

2021 GOALS

INSPIRATION

FOCUS

Use this space for brainstorming.

Use this space for brainstorming.

I WILL PREPARE FOR CHRIST'S DEATH & RESURRECTION BY

Brainstorm and choose what you feel called to commit to during the Lenten Season.

REFLECT

Why did you choose to commit to this?

MY SUPPORT TEAM

Who can help you along the way?

1	2	3	4	5	6	7	8	9	10	11	12	13	14	15	16	17	18	19	20
21	22	23	24	25	26	27	28	29	30	31	32	33	34	35	36	37	38	39	40

Initial after you complete each day.

2021

JANUARY

S	M	T	W	T	F	S
					1	2
3	4	5	6	7	8	9
10	11	12	13	14	15	16
17	18	19	20	21	22	23
24	25	26	27	28	29	30
31						

FEBRUARY

S	M	T	W	T	F	S
	1	2	3	4	5	6
7	8	9	10	11	12	13
14	15	16	17	18	19	20
21	22	23	24	25	26	27
28						

MARCH

S	M	T	W	T	F	S
	1	2	3	4	5	6
7	8	9	10	11	12	13
14	15	16	17	18	19	20
21	22	23	24	25	26	27
28	29	30	31			

APRIL

S	M	T	W	T	F	S
				1	2	3
4	5	6	7	8	9	10
11	12	13	14	15	16	17
18	19	20	21	22	23	24
25	26	27	28	29	30	

MAY

S	M	T	W	T	F	S
						1
2	3	4	5	6	7	8
9	10	11	12	13	14	15
16	17	18	19	20	21	22
23	24	25	26	27	28	29
30	31					

JUNE

S	M	T	W	T	F	S
		1	2	3	4	5
6	7	8	9	10	11	12
13	14	15	16	17	18	19
20	21	22	23	24	25	26
27	28	29	30			

JULY

S	M	T	W	T	F	S
				1	2	3
4	5	6	7	8	9	10
11	12	13	14	15	16	17
18	19	20	21	22	23	24
25	26	27	28	29	30	31

AUGUST

S	M	T	W	T	F	S
1	2	3	4	5	6	7
8	9	10	11	12	13	14
15	16	17	18	19	20	21
22	23	24	25	26	27	28
29	30	31				

SEPTEMBER

S	M	T	W	T	F	S
			1	2	3	4
5	6	7	8	9	10	11
12	13	14	15	16	17	18
19	20	21	22	23	24	25
26	27	28	29	30		

OCTOBER

S	M	T	W	T	F	S
					1	2
3	4	5	6	7	8	9
10	11	12	13	14	15	16
17	18	19	20	21	22	23
24	25	26	27	28	29	30
31						

NOVEMBER

S	M	T	W	T	F	S
	1	2	3	4	5	6
7	8	9	10	11	12	13
14	15	16	17	18	19	20
21	22	23	24	25	26	27
28	29	30				

DECEMBER

S	M	T	W	T	F	S
			1	2	3	4
5	6	7	8	9	10	11
12	13	14	15	16	17	18
19	20	21	22	23	24	25
26	27	28	29	30	31	

<table>
<tr><td>JANUARY</td><td>SUNDAY</td><td>MONDAY</td><td>TUESDAY</td></tr>
<tr><td>NOTES</td><td></td><td></td><td></td></tr>
<tr><td></td><td>3   The Epiphany of the Lord</td><td>4

Saint Elizabeth Ann Seton</td><td>5

Saint John Neumann</td></tr>
<tr><td></td><td>10   The Baptism of the Lord</td><td>11</td><td>12</td></tr>
<tr><td></td><td>17   Second Sunday in Ordinary Time</td><td>18   Martin Luther King, Jr. Day</td><td>19</td></tr>
<tr><td></td><td>24   Third Sunday in Ordinary Time</td><td>25   The Conversion of Saint Paul the Apostle</td><td>26</td></tr>
<tr><td></td><td>31   Fourth Sunday in Ordinary Time</td><td></td><td></td></tr>
</table>

SAINT SEBASTIAN

- Feast Day: January 20
- Born: 256; Died: 288
- Patron saint of soldiers and athletes
- He served in the Roman army to assist other Christians being persecuted by the Romans.
- He was promoted to the Praetorian Guard to protect Emperor Diocletian.

- Twin deacons were arrested for refusing to make public sacrifices. Their parents tried to persuade them to renounce Christianity. Sebastian then converted the parents.
- Sebastian was ordered to be killed by being tied to a post and shot with arrows, but survived.
- He warned Diocletian of his sins and was killed.

<table>
<tr><th>WEDNESDAY</th><th>THURSDAY</th><th>FRIDAY</th><th>SATURDAY</th></tr>
<tr>
<td></td>
<td></td>
<td>1
Solemnity of Mary, the Holy Mother of God

New Year's Day</td>
<td>2

Saints Basil the Great & Gregory Nazianzen</td>
</tr>
<tr>
<td>6

Saint André Bessette</td>
<td>7

Saint Raymond of Penyafort</td>
<td>8</td>
<td>9</td>
</tr>
<tr>
<td>13

Saint Hilary</td>
<td>14</td>
<td>15</td>
<td>16</td>
</tr>
<tr>
<td>20

Saint Fabian
Saint Sebastian</td>
<td>21

Saint Agnes</td>
<td>22
Day of Prayer for the Legal Protection of Unborn Children</td>
<td>23

Saint Vincent
Saint Marianne Cope</td>
</tr>
<tr>
<td>27

Saint Angela Merici</td>
<td>28

Saint Thomas Aquinas</td>
<td>29</td>
<td>30</td>
</tr>
</table>

| READING 1 | READING 2 | GOSPEL |

Sirach 3:2-6, 12-14   Colossians 3:12-21   Luke 2:22-40

Now there was a man in Jerusalem whose name was Simeon. This man was righteous and devout, awaiting the consolation of Israel, and the holy Spirit was upon him. It had been revealed to him by the holy Spirit that he should not see death before he had seen the Messiah of the Lord.

Luke 2:25-26

REFLECTION

HOW WERE YOU IN AWE OF GOD THIS WEEK?

FREE SPACE

HABITS & RITUALS

PRAYER LIST

S M T W T F S

S M T W T F S

S M T W T F S

S M T W T F S

S M T W T F S

| | SUNDAY 27 | MONDAY 28 | TUESDAY 29 |

PRIORITIES

MORNING

MORNING

MORNING

DAY

DAY

DAY

NIGHT

NIGHT

NIGHT

NOTES

<table>
<tr><th>WEDNESDAY
30</th><th>THURSDAY
31</th><th>FRIDAY
1</th><th>SATURDAY
2</th></tr>
<tr><td>MORNING</td><td>MORNING</td><td>**Solemnity of Mary**
New Year's Day</td><td>MORNING</td></tr>
<tr><td>DAY</td><td>DAY</td><td>DAY</td><td>DAY</td></tr>
<tr><td>NIGHT</td><td>NIGHT</td><td>NIGHT</td><td>NIGHT</td></tr>
</table>

READING 1	READING 2	GOSPEL
Isaiah 60:1-6	Ephesians 3:2-3a, 5-6	Matthew 2:1-12

They were overjoyed at seeing the star, and on entering the house they saw the child with Mary his mother. They prostrated themselves and did him homage. Then they opened their treasures and offered him gifts of gold, frankincense, and myrrh.

Matthew 2:10-11

REFLECTION

HOW WERE YOU IN AWE OF GOD THIS WEEK?

FREE SPACE

HABITS & RITUALS

PRAYER LIST

S M T W T F S

S M T W T F S

S M T W T F S

S M T W T F S

S M T W T F S

| SUNDAY 3 | MONDAY 4 | TUESDAY 5 |

PRIORITIES

SUNDAY 3 — The Epiphany of the Lord

MORNING / DAY / NIGHT

MONDAY 4 — MORNING / DAY / NIGHT

TUESDAY 5 — MORNING / DAY / NIGHT

NOTES

<table>
<tr><th>WEDNESDAY
6</th><th>THURSDAY
7</th><th>FRIDAY
8</th><th>SATURDAY
9</th></tr>
<tr><td>MORNING</td><td>MORNING</td><td>MORNING</td><td>MORNING</td></tr>
<tr><td>DAY</td><td>DAY</td><td>DAY</td><td>DAY</td></tr>
<tr><td>NIGHT</td><td>NIGHT</td><td>NIGHT</td><td>NIGHT</td></tr>
</table>

TO DO   **LIST**

READING 1	READING 2	GOSPEL
Isaiah 42:1-4, 6-7	Acts 10:34-38	Mark 1:7-11

It happened in those days that Jesus came from Nazareth of Galilee and was baptized in the Jordan by John. On coming up out of the water he saw the heavens being torn open and the Spirit, like a dove, descending upon him. And a voice came from the heavens, "You are my beloved Son; with you I am well pleased."

Mark 1:9-11

REFLECTION

HOW WERE YOU IN AWE OF GOD THIS WEEK?

FREE SPACE

HABITS & RITUALS

S M T W T F S

S M T W T F S

S M T W T F S

S M T W T F S

S M T W T F S

PRAYER LIST

PRIORITIES	SUNDAY 10	MONDAY 11	TUESDAY 12
	The Baptism of the Lord	MORNING	MORNING
	DAY	DAY	DAY
	NIGHT	NIGHT	NIGHT

NOTES

<table>
<tr><th>WEDNESDAY
13</th><th>THURSDAY
14</th><th>FRIDAY
15</th><th>SATURDAY
16</th></tr>
<tr><td>MORNING</td><td>MORNING</td><td>MORNING</td><td>MORNING</td></tr>
<tr><td>DAY</td><td>DAY</td><td>DAY</td><td>DAY</td></tr>
<tr><td>NIGHT</td><td>NIGHT</td><td>NIGHT</td><td>NIGHT</td></tr>
</table>

TO DO

LIST

READING 1	READING 2	GOSPEL
1 Samuel 3:3b-10, 19	1 Cor 6:13c-15a, 17-20	John 1:35-42

The next day John was there again with two of his disciples, and as he watched Jesus walk by, he said, "Behold, the Lamb of God." The two disciples heard what he said and followed Jesus.

John 1:35-37

REFLECTION

HOW WERE YOU IN AWE OF GOD THIS WEEK?

FREE SPACE

HABITS & RITUALS

PRAYER LIST

S	M	T	W	T	F	S

S	M	T	W	T	F	S

S	M	T	W	T	F	S

S	M	T	W	T	F	S

S	M	T	W	T	F	S

SUNDAY 17	MONDAY 18	TUESDAY 19
MORNING	*Martin Luther King, Jr. Day*	MORNING
DAY	DAY	DAY
NIGHT	NIGHT	NIGHT

NOTES

<table>
<tr><th>WEDNESDAY 20</th><th>THURSDAY 21</th><th>FRIDAY 22</th><th>SATURDAY 23</th></tr>
<tr><td>MORNING</td><td>MORNING</td><td>MORNING</td><td>MORNING</td></tr>
<tr><td>DAY</td><td>DAY</td><td>DAY</td><td>DAY</td></tr>
<tr><td>NIGHT</td><td>NIGHT</td><td>NIGHT</td><td>NIGHT</td></tr>
</table>

TO DO

LIST

READING 1	READING 2	GOSPEL
Jonah 3:1-5, 10	1 Corinthians 7:29-31	Mark 1:14-20

After John had been arrested, Jesus came to Galilee proclaiming the gospel of God: "This is the time of fulfillment. The kingdom of God is at hand. Repent, and believe in the gospel."

Mark 1:14-15

REFLECTION

HOW WERE YOU IN AWE OF GOD THIS WEEK?

FREE SPACE

HABITS & RITUALS

PRAYER LIST

S M T W T F S

S M T W T F S

S M T W T F S

S M T W T F S

S M T W T F S

JANUARY

PRIORITIES

SUNDAY
24

MONDAY
25

TUESDAY
26

MORNING

MORNING

MORNING

DAY

DAY

DAY

NIGHT

NIGHT

NIGHT

NOTES

<table>
<tr><td>WEDNESDAY
27</td><td>THURSDAY
28</td><td>FRIDAY
29</td><td>SATURDAY
30</td></tr>
<tr><td>MORNING</td><td>MORNING</td><td>MORNING</td><td>MORNING</td></tr>
<tr><td>DAY</td><td>DAY</td><td>DAY</td><td>DAY</td></tr>
<tr><td>NIGHT</td><td>NIGHT</td><td>NIGHT</td><td>NIGHT</td></tr>
</table>

TO DO

LIST

FEBRUARY	SUNDAY	MONDAY	TUESDAY
NOTES		1	2 The Presentation of the Lord
	7 Fifth Sunday in Ordinary Time	8 Saint Jerome Emiliani Saint Josephine Bakhita	9
	14 Sixth Sunday in Ordinary Time *Valentine's Day*	15 *President's Day*	16
	21 First Sunday of Lent	22 The Chair of Saint Peter the Apostle	23 Saint Polycarp
	28 Second Sunday of Lent		

SAINT DOROTHY

- Feast Day: February 6
- Born: c.279–290; Died: c.311
- Patron saint of brewers, brides, florists, gardeners, and newlyweds
- She suffered persecution under Emperor Diocletian and was tortured and sentenced to death.

- On her way to execution, a pagan lawyer mocked her by telling her to send fruits from Christ's garden that she would soon be in.
- She sent her headdress to him before her execution, which was found filled with fruits and roses.
- The pagan lawyer, Theophilus, then converted.

<table>
<thead>
<tr><th>WEDNESDAY</th><th>THURSDAY</th><th>FRIDAY</th><th>SATURDAY</th></tr>
</thead>
<tbody>
<tr><td>3

Saint Blaise
Saint Ansgar</td><td>4</td><td>5

Saint Agatha</td><td>6

Saint Paul Miki & Companions
Saint Dorothy</td></tr>
<tr><td>10

Saint Scholastica</td><td>11   Our Lady of Lourdes</td><td>12</td><td>13</td></tr>
<tr><td>17   Ash Wednesday</td><td>18</td><td>19</td><td>20</td></tr>
<tr><td>24</td><td>25</td><td>26</td><td>27</td></tr>
<tr><td></td><td></td><td></td><td></td></tr>
</tbody>
</table>

GOALS

| READING 1 | READING 2 | GOSPEL |

Deuteronomy 18:15-20   1 Corinthians 7:32-35   Mark 1:21-28

The unclean spirit convulsed him and with a loud cry came out of him. All were amazed and asked one another, "What is this? A new teaching with authority. He commands even the unclean spirits and they obey him." His fame spread everywhere throughout the whole region of Galilee.

Mark 1:26-28

REFLECTION

HOW WERE YOU IN AWE OF GOD THIS WEEK?

<table>
<tr><td>JAN & FEB</td><td>SUNDAY
31</td><td>MONDAY
1</td><td>TUESDAY
2</td></tr>
<tr><td>PRIORITIES</td><td>MORNING</td><td>MORNING</td><td>MORNING</td></tr>
<tr><td></td><td>DAY</td><td>DAY</td><td>DAY</td></tr>
<tr><td></td><td>NIGHT</td><td>NIGHT</td><td>NIGHT</td></tr>
</table>

NOTES

<table>
<tr><td>WEDNESDAY
3</td><td>THURSDAY
4</td><td>FRIDAY
5</td><td>SATURDAY
6</td></tr>
<tr><td>MORNING</td><td>MORNING</td><td>MORNING</td><td>MORNING</td></tr>
<tr><td>DAY</td><td>DAY</td><td>DAY</td><td>DAY</td></tr>
<tr><td>NIGHT</td><td>NIGHT</td><td>NIGHT</td><td>NIGHT</td></tr>
</table>

TO DO

- [ ]
- [ ]
- [ ]
- [ ]
- [ ]
- [ ]
- [ ]
- [ ]
- [ ]
- [ ]

LIST

- [ ]
- [ ]
- [ ]
- [ ]
- [ ]
- [ ]
- [ ]
- [ ]
- [ ]
- [ ]

READING 1	READING 2	GOSPEL
Job 7:1-4, 6-7	1 Cor 9:16-19, 22-23	Mark 1:29-39

He told them, "Let us go on to the nearby villages that I may preach there also. For this purpose have I come." So he went into their synagogues, preaching and driving out demons throughout the whole of Galilee.

Mark 1:38-39

REFLECTION

HOW WERE YOU IN AWE OF GOD THIS WEEK?

FREE SPACE

HABITS & RITUALS

| S | M | T | W | T | F | S |

| S | M | T | W | T | F | S |

| S | M | T | W | T | F | S |

| S | M | T | W | T | F | S |

| S | M | T | W | T | F | S |

PRAYER LIST

<table><tr><td>FEBRUARY</td><td>SUNDAY 7</td><td>MONDAY 8</td><td>TUESDAY 9</td></tr></table>

PRIORITIES

	MORNING	MORNING	MORNING
	DAY	DAY	DAY
	NIGHT	NIGHT	NIGHT

NOTES

<table>
<tr><th>WEDNESDAY
10</th><th>THURSDAY
11</th><th>FRIDAY
12</th><th>SATURDAY
13</th></tr>
<tr><td>MORNING</td><td>MORNING</td><td>MORNING</td><td>MORNING</td></tr>
<tr><td>DAY</td><td>DAY</td><td>DAY</td><td>DAY</td></tr>
<tr><td>NIGHT</td><td>NIGHT</td><td>NIGHT</td><td>NIGHT</td></tr>
</table>

TO DO

LIST

READING 1	READING 2	GOSPEL
Leviticus 13:1-2, 44-46	1 Corinthians 10:31—11:1	Mark 1:40-45

The man went away and began to publicize the whole matter. He spread the report abroad so that it was impossible for Jesus to enter a town openly. He remained outside in deserted places, and people kept coming to him from everywhere.

Mark 1:45

REFLECTION

HOW WERE YOU IN AWE OF GOD THIS WEEK?

FREE SPACE

HABITS & RITUALS

PRAYER LIST

S M T W T F S

S M T W T F S

S M T W T F S

S M T W T F S

S M T W T F S

FEBRUARY	SUNDAY 14	MONDAY 15	TUESDAY 16
PRIORITIES	*Valentine's Day*	*President's Day*	MORNING
	DAY	DAY	DAY
	NIGHT	NIGHT	NIGHT

NOTES

<table>
<tr><th>WEDNESDAY 17</th><th>THURSDAY 18</th><th>FRIDAY 19</th><th>SATURDAY 20</th></tr>
<tr><td>Ash Wednesday</td><td>MORNING</td><td>MORNING</td><td>MORNING</td></tr>
<tr><td>DAY</td><td>DAY</td><td>DAY</td><td>DAY</td></tr>
<tr><td>NIGHT</td><td>NIGHT</td><td>NIGHT</td><td>NIGHT</td></tr>
</table>

TO DO

- ☐
- ☐
- ☐
- ☐
- ☐
- ☐
- ☐
- ☐
- ☐
- ☐

LIST

- ☐
- ☐
- ☐
- ☐
- ☐
- ☐
- ☐
- ☐
- ☐
- ☐

READING 1	READING 2	GOSPEL
Genesis 9:8-15	1 Peter 3:18-22	Mark 1:12-15

At once the Spirit drove him out into the desert, and he remained in the desert for forty days, tempted by Satan. He was among wild beasts, and the angels ministered to him.

Mark 1:12-13

REFLECTION

HOW WERE YOU IN AWE OF GOD THIS WEEK?

FREE SPACE

HABITS & RITUALS

PRAYER LIST

| S | M | T | W | T | F | S |

| S | M | T | W | T | F | S |

| S | M | T | W | T | F | S |

| S | M | T | W | T | F | S |

| S | M | T | W | T | F | S |

SUNDAY 21	MONDAY 22	TUESDAY 23

PRIORITIES

SUNDAY 21
MORNING
DAY
NIGHT

MONDAY 22
MORNING
DAY
NIGHT

TUESDAY 23
MORNING
DAY
NIGHT

NOTES

<table>
<tr><th>WEDNESDAY
24</th><th>THURSDAY
25</th><th>FRIDAY
26</th><th>SATURDAY
27</th></tr>
<tr><td>MORNING</td><td>MORNING</td><td>MORNING</td><td>MORNING</td></tr>
<tr><td>DAY</td><td>DAY</td><td>DAY</td><td>DAY</td></tr>
<tr><td>NIGHT</td><td>NIGHT</td><td>NIGHT</td><td>NIGHT</td></tr>
</table>

TO DO

LIST

<table>
<tr><td>MARCH</td><td>SUNDAY</td><td>MONDAY</td><td>TUESDAY</td></tr>
<tr><td>NOTES</td><td></td><td>1</td><td>2</td></tr>
<tr><td></td><td>7   Third Sunday of Lent</td><td>8

Saint John of God</td><td>9

Saint Frances of Rome</td></tr>
<tr><td></td><td>14   Fourth Sunday of Lent
Daylight Saving Time</td><td>15</td><td>16</td></tr>
<tr><td></td><td>21   Fifth Sunday of Lent

Saint Nicholas of Flüe</td><td>22</td><td>23

Saint Turibius of Mogrovejo</td></tr>
<tr><td></td><td>28   Palm Sunday of the Passion of the Lord</td><td>29</td><td>30</td></tr>
</table>

SAINT NICHOLAS OF FLÜE

- Feast Day: March 21
- Born: c.1417-1421; Died: March 1487
- Patron saint of Switzerland
- He was a military leader who fought with a sword in one hard and a rosary in the other.
- After receiving a mystical vision of a lily eaten by a horse, he took up the life of a hermit.
- He is said to have survived for nineteen years with no food except for the Holy Eucharist.
- He was visited by those who sought spiritual council throughout Europe.
- His intervention in a conflict over the admission of Fribourg and Solothurn to the Swiss Confederation helped prevent civil war.

<table>
<tr><td>WEDNESDAY</td><td>THURSDAY</td><td>FRIDAY</td><td>SATURDAY</td></tr>
<tr><td>3

Saint Katharine Drexel</td><td>4

Saint Casimir</td><td>5</td><td>6</td></tr>
<tr><td>10</td><td>11</td><td>12</td><td>13</td></tr>
<tr><td>17

Saint Patrick</td><td>18

Saint Cyril of Jerusalem</td><td>19 Saint Joseph, Spouse of the Blessed Virgin Mary</td><td>20</td></tr>
<tr><td>24</td><td>25 The Annunciation of the Lord</td><td>26</td><td>27</td></tr>
<tr><td>31</td><td></td><td></td><td></td></tr>
</table>

READING 1	READING 2	GOSPEL
Gen 22:1-2, 9a, 10-13, 15-18	Romans 8:31b-34	Mark 9:2-10

After six days Jesus took Peter, James, and John and led them up a high mountain apart by themselves. And he was transfigured before them, and his clothes became dazzling white, such as no fuller on earth could bleach them.

Mark 9:2-3

REFLECTION

HOW WERE YOU IN AWE OF GOD THIS WEEK?

FREE SPACE

HABITS & RITUALS

S M T W T F S

S M T W T F S

S M T W T F S

S M T W T F S

S M T W T F S

PRAYER LIST

<table>
<tr><td>FEB & MAR</td><td>SUNDAY
28</td><td>MONDAY
1</td><td>TUESDAY
2</td></tr>
<tr><td>PRIORITIES</td><td>MORNING</td><td>MORNING</td><td>MORNING</td></tr>
<tr><td></td><td>DAY</td><td>DAY</td><td>DAY</td></tr>
<tr><td></td><td>NIGHT</td><td>NIGHT</td><td>NIGHT</td></tr>
</table>

NOTES

<table>
<tr><th>WEDNESDAY
3</th><th>THURSDAY
4</th><th>FRIDAY
5</th><th>SATURDAY
6</th></tr>
<tr><td>MORNING</td><td>MORNING</td><td>MORNING</td><td>MORNING</td></tr>
<tr><td>DAY</td><td>DAY</td><td>DAY</td><td>DAY</td></tr>
<tr><td>NIGHT</td><td>NIGHT</td><td>NIGHT</td><td>NIGHT</td></tr>
</table>

TO DO **LIST**

READING 1	READING 2	GOSPEL
Exodus 20:1-17	1 Corinthians 1:22-25	John 2:13-25

Jesus answered and said to them, "Destroy this temple and in three days I will raise it up." The Jews said, "This temple has been under construction for forty-six years, and you will raise it up in three days?" But he was speaking about the temple of his body.

John 2:19-21

REFLECTION

HOW WERE YOU IN AWE OF GOD THIS WEEK?

FREE SPACE

HABITS & RITUALS

PRAYER LIST

| S | M | T | W | T | F | S |

| S | M | T | W | T | F | S |

| S | M | T | W | T | F | S |

| S | M | T | W | T | F | S |

| S | M | T | W | T | F | S |

SUNDAY	MONDAY	TUESDAY
7	8	9

PRIORITIES

7 SUNDAY

MORNING

DAY

NIGHT

8 MONDAY

MORNING

DAY

NIGHT

9 TUESDAY

MORNING

DAY

NIGHT

NOTES

<table>
<tr><td>WEDNESDAY
10</td><td>THURSDAY
11</td><td>FRIDAY
12</td><td>SATURDAY
13</td></tr>
<tr><td>MORNING</td><td>MORNING</td><td>MORNING</td><td>MORNING</td></tr>
<tr><td>DAY</td><td>DAY</td><td>DAY</td><td>DAY</td></tr>
<tr><td>NIGHT</td><td>NIGHT</td><td>NIGHT</td><td>NIGHT</td></tr>
</table>

TO DO

LIST

READING 1	READING 2	GOSPEL
2 Chr 36:14-16, 19-23	Ephesians 2:4-10	John 3:14-21

For God so loved the world that he gave his only Son, so that everyone who believes in him might not perish but might have eternal life. For God did not send his Son into the world to condemn the world, but that the world might be saved through him.

John 3:16-17

REFLECTION

HOW WERE YOU IN AWE OF GOD THIS WEEK?

FREE SPACE

HABITS & RITUALS

PRAYER LIST

S M T W T F S

S M T W T F S

S M T W T F S

S M T W T F S

S M T W T F S

<table>
<tr><td>MARCH</td><td>SUNDAY 14</td><td>MONDAY 15</td><td>TUESDAY 16</td></tr>
</table>

PRIORITIES

	SUNDAY 14	MONDAY 15	TUESDAY 16
	Daylight Saving Time	MORNING	MORNING
	DAY	DAY	DAY
	NIGHT	NIGHT	NIGHT

NOTES

<table>
<tr><th>WEDNESDAY
17</th><th>THURSDAY
18</th><th>FRIDAY
19</th><th>SATURDAY
20</th></tr>
<tr><td>MORNING</td><td>MORNING</td><td>Saint Joseph, Spouse of the Blessed Virgin Mary</td><td>MORNING</td></tr>
<tr><td>DAY</td><td>DAY</td><td>DAY</td><td>DAY</td></tr>
<tr><td>NIGHT</td><td>NIGHT</td><td>NIGHT</td><td>NIGHT</td></tr>
</table>

TO DO LIST

READING 1	READING 2	GOSPEL
Jeremiah 31:31-34	Hebrews 5:7-9	John 12:20-33

Amen, amen, I say to you, unless a grain of wheat falls to the ground and dies, it remains just a grain of wheat; but if it dies, it produces much fruit. Whoever loves his life loses it, and whoever hates his life in this world will preserve it for eternal life.

John 12:24-25

REFLECTION

HOW WERE YOU IN AWE OF GOD THIS WEEK?

WEEKLY RETREAT

FREE SPACE

HABITS & RITUALS

PRAYER LIST

S M T W T F S
S M T W T F S
S M T W T F S
S M T W T F S
S M T W T F S

<table>
<tr><td>MARCH</td><td>SUNDAY 21</td><td>MONDAY 22</td><td>TUESDAY 23</td></tr>
<tr><td>PRIORITIES</td><td>MORNING</td><td>MORNING</td><td>MORNING</td></tr>
<tr><td></td><td>DAY</td><td>DAY</td><td>DAY</td></tr>
<tr><td></td><td>NIGHT</td><td>NIGHT</td><td>NIGHT</td></tr>
</table>

NOTES

<table>
<tr><th>WEDNESDAY 24</th><th>THURSDAY 25</th><th>FRIDAY 26</th><th>SATURDAY 27</th></tr>
<tr><td>MORNING</td><td>The Annunciation of the Lord</td><td>MORNING</td><td>MORNING</td></tr>
<tr><td>DAY</td><td>DAY</td><td>DAY</td><td>DAY</td></tr>
<tr><td>NIGHT</td><td>NIGHT</td><td>NIGHT</td><td>NIGHT</td></tr>
</table>

TO DO LIST

NOTES

	4 Easter Sunday	**5**	**6**
	11 Second Sunday of Easter (Sunday of Divine Mercy) *Saint Gemma Galgani*	**12**	**13** *Saint Martin I*
	18 Third Sunday of Easter	**19**	**20**
	25 Fourth Sunday of Easter	**26**	**27**

SAINT GEMMA GALGANI

- Feast Day: April 11
- Born: 1878; Died: April 11, 1903
- Patron saint of students, pharmacists, against temptation, and against loss of parents
- She was known as the "Flower of Lucca."
- She attended a Catholic boarding school and developed a love for prayer at a young age.

- She developed spinal meningitis at the age of 16 and prayed to the Sacred Heart of Jesus.
- At the age of 16, she became the mother figure to her younger siblings when her father died.
- She experienced stigmata at the age of 21.
- She often saw and spoke to her guardian angel, Jesus, Mary, and other saints.

WEDNESDAY	THURSDAY	FRIDAY	SATURDAY
	1 — *Holy Thursday*	2 — *Good Friday* — Saint Francis of Paola	3 — *Holy Saturday*
7 — Saint John Baptist de la Salle	8	9	10
14	15 — *Tax Day*	16 — Saint Bernadette	17
21 — Saint Anselm	22 — *Earth Day*	23 — Saint George / Saint Adalbert	24 — Saint Fidelis of Sigmaringen
28 — Saint Peter Chanel / Saint Louis Grignion de Montfort	29 — Saint Catherine of Siena	30 — Saint Pius V	

GOALS

READING 1	READING 2	GOSPEL
Isaiah 50:4-7	Philippians 2:6-11	Mark 14:1—15:47

Then Judas Iscariot, one of the Twelve, went off to the chief priests to hand him over to them. When they heard him they were pleased and promised to pay him money. Then he looked for an opportunity to hand him over.

Mark 14:10-11

REFLECTION

HOW WERE YOU IN AWE OF GOD THIS WEEK?

FREE SPACE

HABITS & RITUALS

PRAYER LIST

S M T W T F S

S M T W T F S

S M T W T F S

S M T W T F S

S M T W T F S

	SUNDAY 28	MONDAY 29	TUESDAY 30
PRIORITIES	Palm Sunday	MORNING	MORNING
	DAY	DAY	DAY
	NIGHT	NIGHT	NIGHT

NOTES

<table>
<tr><td>WEDNESDAY
31</td><td>THURSDAY
1</td><td>FRIDAY
2</td><td>SATURDAY
3</td></tr>
<tr><td>MORNING</td><td>Holy Thursday</td><td>Good Friday</td><td>Holy Saturday</td></tr>
<tr><td>DAY</td><td>DAY</td><td>DAY</td><td>DAY</td></tr>
<tr><td>NIGHT</td><td>NIGHT</td><td>NIGHT</td><td>NIGHT</td></tr>
</table>

TO DO

LIST

READING 1	READING 2	GOSPEL
Acts 10:34a, 37-43	Colossians 3:1-4	John 20:1-9

When Simon Peter arrived after him, he went into the tomb and saw the burial cloths there, and the cloth that had covered his head, not with the burial cloths but rolled up in a separate place. Then the other disciple also went in, the one who had arrived at the tomb first, and he saw and believed.

John 20:6-8

REFLECTION

HOW WERE YOU IN AWE OF GOD THIS WEEK?

WEEKLY RETREAT

FREE SPACE

HABITS & RITUALS

S	M	T	W	T	F	S
S	M	T	W	T	F	S
S	M	T	W	T	F	S
S	M	T	W	T	F	S
S	M	T	W	T	F	S

PRAYER LIST

APRIL	SUNDAY 4	MONDAY 5	TUESDAY 6

PRIORITIES

	Easter Sunday	MORNING	MORNING
	DAY	DAY	DAY
	NIGHT	NIGHT	NIGHT

NOTES

WEDNESDAY
7
THURSDAY
8
FRIDAY
9
SATURDAY
10
MORNING
MORNING
MORNING
MORNING
DAY
DAY
DAY
DAY
NIGHT
NIGHT
NIGHT
NIGHT
TO DO
LIST

READING 1	READING 2	GOSPEL
Acts 4:32-35	1 John 5:1-6	John 20:19-31

Thomas, called Didymus, one of the Twelve, was not with them when Jesus came. So the other disciples said to him, "We have seen the Lord." But he said to them, "Unless I see the mark of the nails in his hands and put my finger into the nailmarks and put my hand into his side, I will not believe."

John 20:24-25

REFLECTION

HOW WERE YOU IN AWE OF GOD THIS WEEK?

FREE SPACE

HABITS & RITUALS

PRAYER LIST

S M T W T F S

S M T W T F S

S M T W T F S

S M T W T F S

S M T W T F S

<table>
<tr><td>APRIL</td><td>SUNDAY 11</td><td>MONDAY 12</td><td>TUESDAY 13</td></tr>
<tr><td>PRIORITIES</td><td>Sunday of Divine Mercy</td><td>MORNING</td><td>MORNING</td></tr>
<tr><td></td><td>DAY</td><td>DAY</td><td>DAY</td></tr>
<tr><td></td><td>NIGHT</td><td>NIGHT</td><td>NIGHT</td></tr>
</table>

NOTES

<table>
<tr><th>WEDNESDAY 14</th><th>THURSDAY 15</th><th>FRIDAY 16</th><th>SATURDAY 17</th></tr>
<tr><td>MORNING</td><td>*Tax Day*</td><td>MORNING</td><td>MORNING</td></tr>
<tr><td>DAY</td><td>DAY</td><td>DAY</td><td>DAY</td></tr>
<tr><td>NIGHT</td><td>NIGHT</td><td>NIGHT</td><td>NIGHT</td></tr>
</table>

TO DO

- [ ]
- [ ]
- [ ]
- [ ]
- [ ]
- [ ]
- [ ]
- [ ]
- [ ]
- [ ]

LIST

- [ ]
- [ ]
- [ ]
- [ ]
- [ ]
- [ ]
- [ ]
- [ ]
- [ ]
- [ ]

| READING 1 | READING 2 | GOSPEL |

Acts 3:13-15, 17-19   1 John 2:1-5a   Luke 24:35-48

After three days they found him in the temple, sitting in the midst of the teachers, listening to them and asking them questions, and all who heard him were astounded at his understanding and his answers.

Luke 2:46-47

REFLECTION

HOW WERE YOU IN AWE OF GOD THIS WEEK?

FREE SPACE

HABITS & RITUALS	PRAYER LIST

S M T W T F S

S M T W T F S

S M T W T F S

S M T W T F S

S M T W T F S

<table>
<tr><td>APRIL</td><td>SUNDAY 18</td><td>MONDAY 19</td><td>TUESDAY 20</td></tr>
<tr><td>PRIORITIES</td><td>MORNING</td><td>MORNING</td><td>MORNING</td></tr>
<tr><td></td><td>DAY</td><td>DAY</td><td>DAY</td></tr>
<tr><td></td><td>NIGHT</td><td>NIGHT</td><td>NIGHT</td></tr>
</table>

NOTES

<table>
<tr><td>WEDNESDAY
21</td><td>THURSDAY
22</td><td>FRIDAY
23</td><td>SATURDAY
24</td></tr>
<tr><td>MORNING</td><td>*Earth Day*</td><td>MORNING</td><td>MORNING</td></tr>
<tr><td>DAY</td><td>DAY</td><td>DAY</td><td>DAY</td></tr>
<tr><td>NIGHT</td><td>NIGHT</td><td>NIGHT</td><td>NIGHT</td></tr>
</table>

TO DO

LIST

<table>
<tr><th>MAY</th><th>SUNDAY</th><th>MONDAY</th><th>TUESDAY</th></tr>
<tr><td>NOTES</td><td></td><td></td><td></td></tr>
<tr><td></td><td>2 Fifth Sunday of Easter</td><td>3

Saints Philip & James</td><td>4</td></tr>
<tr><td></td><td>9 Sixth Sunday of Easter
Mother's Day</td><td>10

Saint Damien de Veuster</td><td>11</td></tr>
<tr><td></td><td>16 The Ascension of the Lord/ Seventh Sunday of Easter*</td><td>17</td><td>18

Saint John I</td></tr>
<tr><td></td><td>23 Pentecost Sunday</td><td>24 The Blessed Virgin Mary, Mother of the Church
Victoria Day (CA)</td><td>25</td></tr>
<tr><td></td><td>30 The Most Holy Trinity</td><td>31 The Visitation of the Blessed Virgin Mary
Memorial Day</td><td>Saint Bede the Venerable
Saint Gregory VII
Saint Mary Magdalene de' Pazzi</td></tr>
</table>

SAINT MARY MAGDALENE DE' PAZZI

- Feast Day: May 25
- Born: April 2, 1566; Died: March 25, 1607
- Patron saint of sick people and against temptation
- She was born to one of the wealthiest noble families of Renaissance Florence.
- She took a vow of virginity at a young age.
- She experienced her first religious ecstasy at the age of 12 and continued to exhibit many mystical experiences thereafter.
- She was educated at a monastery of nuns.
- During her ecstasies, she dictated her experiences to her fellow nuns and filled five large books over six years.

<table>
<tr><th>WEDNESDAY</th><th>THURSDAY</th><th>FRIDAY</th><th>SATURDAY</th></tr>
<tr><td></td><td></td><td></td><td>1

Saint Joseph the Worker</td></tr>
<tr><td>5</td><td>6</td><td>7</td><td>8</td></tr>
<tr><td>12

Saints Nereus & Achilleus
Saint Pancras</td><td>13
The Ascension of the Lord*</td><td>14

Saint Matthias</td><td>15

Saint Isidore
Saint Dymphna</td></tr>
<tr><td>19</td><td>20

Saint Bernadine of Siena</td><td>21

Saint Christopher Magallanes & Companions</td><td>22

Saint Rita of Cascia</td></tr>
<tr><td>26

Saint Philip Neri</td><td>27

Saint Augustine of Canterbury</td><td>28</td><td>29

Saint Paul VI</td></tr>
</table>

*Ecclesiastical Provinces of Boston, Hartford, New York, Newark, Omaha, Philadelphia

GOALS

READING 1	READING 2	GOSPEL
Acts 4:8-12	1 John 3:1-2	John 10:11-18

I am the good shepherd. A good shepherd lays down his life for the sheep. A hired man, who is not a shepherd and whose sheep are not his own, sees a wolf coming and leaves the sheep and runs away, and the wolf catches and scatters them. This is because he works for pay and has no concern for the sheep.

John 10:11-13

REFLECTION

HOW WERE YOU IN AWE OF GOD THIS WEEK?

FREE SPACE

HABITS & RITUALS

PRAYER LIST

S M T W T F S

S M T W T F S

S M T W T F S

S M T W T F S

S M T W T F S

APR & MAY	SUNDAY 25	MONDAY 26	TUESDAY 27
PRIORITIES	MORNING	MORNING	MORNING
	DAY	DAY	DAY
	NIGHT	NIGHT	NIGHT

NOTES

<table>
<tr><td>WEDNESDAY
28</td><td>THURSDAY
29</td><td>FRIDAY
30</td><td>SATURDAY
1</td></tr>
<tr><td>MORNING</td><td>MORNING</td><td>MORNING</td><td>MORNING</td></tr>
<tr><td>DAY</td><td>DAY</td><td>DAY</td><td>DAY</td></tr>
<tr><td>NIGHT</td><td>NIGHT</td><td>NIGHT</td><td>NIGHT</td></tr>
</table>

TO DO **LIST**

READING 1	READING 2	GOSPEL
Acts 9:26-31	1 John 3:18-24	John 15:1-8

Remain in me, as I remain in you. Just as a branch cannot bear fruit on its own unless it remains on the vine, so neither can you unless you remain in me. I am the vine, you are the branches. Whoever remains in me and I in him will bear much fruit, because without me you can do nothing.

John 15:4-5

REFLECTION

HOW WERE YOU IN AWE OF GOD THIS WEEK?

WEEKLY RETREAT

FREE SPACE

HABITS & RITUALS

PRAYER LIST

S M T W T F S
S M T W T F S
S M T W T F S
S M T W T F S
S M T W T F S

<table>
<tr><td>MAY</td><td>SUNDAY
2</td><td>MONDAY
3</td><td>TUESDAY
4</td></tr>
<tr><td>PRIORITIES</td><td>MORNING</td><td>MORNING</td><td>MORNING</td></tr>
<tr><td></td><td>DAY</td><td>DAY</td><td>DAY</td></tr>
<tr><td></td><td>NIGHT</td><td>NIGHT</td><td>NIGHT</td></tr>
</table>

NOTES

<table>
<tr><th>WEDNESDAY</th><th>THURSDAY</th><th>FRIDAY</th><th>SATURDAY</th></tr>
<tr><td>5</td><td>6</td><td>7</td><td>8</td></tr>
</table>

MORNING	MORNING	MORNING	MORNING
DAY	DAY	DAY	DAY
NIGHT	NIGHT	NIGHT	NIGHT

TO DO

LIST

READING 1	READING 2	GOSPEL
Acts 10:25-26, 34-35, 44-48	1 John 4:7-10	John 15:9-17

As the Father loves me, so I also love you. Remain in my love. If you keep my commandments, you will remain in my love, just as I have kept my Father's commandments and remain in his love. I have told you this so that my joy may be in you and your joy may be complete. This is my commandment: love one another as I love you.

John 15:9-12

REFLECTION

HOW WERE YOU IN AWE OF GOD THIS WEEK?

FREE SPACE

<table>
<tr><td>HABITS & RITUALS</td><td>PRAYER LIST</td></tr>
</table>

S | M | T | W | T | F | S

S | M | T | W | T | F | S

S | M | T | W | T | F | S

S | M | T | W | T | F | S

S | M | T | W | T | F | S

SUNDAY 9	MONDAY 10	TUESDAY 11

PRIORITIES

SUNDAY 9

Mother's Day

MONDAY 10

MORNING

TUESDAY 11

MORNING

DAY

DAY

DAY

NIGHT

NIGHT

NIGHT

NOTES

<table>
<tr><th>WEDNESDAY
12</th><th>THURSDAY
13</th><th>FRIDAY
14</th><th>SATURDAY
15</th></tr>
<tr><td>MORNING</td><td>**The Ascension of the Lord***</td><td>MORNING</td><td>MORNING</td></tr>
<tr><td>DAY</td><td>DAY</td><td>DAY</td><td>DAY</td></tr>
<tr><td>NIGHT</td><td>NIGHT</td><td>NIGHT</td><td>NIGHT</td></tr>
</table>

TO DO

LIST

READING 1	READING 2	GOSPEL
Acts 1:1-11	Ephesians 1:17-23	Mark 16:15-20

These signs will accompany those who believe: in my name they will drive out demons, they will speak new languages. They will pick up serpents [with their hands], and if they drink any deadly thing, it will not harm them. They will lay hands on the sick, and they will recover."

Mark 16:17-18

REFLECTION

HOW WERE YOU IN AWE OF GOD THIS WEEK?

WEEKLY RETREAT

FREE SPACE

HABITS & RITUALS

PRAYER LIST

S M T W T F S
S M T W T F S
S M T W T F S
S M T W T F S
S M T W T F S

<table>
<tr><td>MAY</td><td>SUNDAY 16</td><td>MONDAY 17</td><td>TUESDAY 18</td></tr>
</table>

PRIORITIES

SUNDAY 16 — The Ascension of the Lord

	MORNING	MORNING
DAY	DAY	DAY
NIGHT	NIGHT	NIGHT

NOTES

<table>
<tr><th>WEDNESDAY 19</th><th>THURSDAY 20</th><th>FRIDAY 21</th><th>SATURDAY 22</th></tr>
<tr><td>MORNING</td><td>MORNING</td><td>MORNING</td><td>MORNING</td></tr>
<tr><td>DAY</td><td>DAY</td><td>DAY</td><td>DAY</td></tr>
<tr><td>NIGHT</td><td>NIGHT</td><td>NIGHT</td><td>NIGHT</td></tr>
</table>

TO DO

LIST

READING 1	READING 2	GOSPEL
Genesis 11:1-9	Romans 8:22-27	John 7:37-39

On the last and greatest day of the feast, Jesus stood up and exclaimed, "Let anyone who thirsts come to me and drink.
Whoever believes in me, as scripture says:
'Rivers of living water will flow from within him.'"

John 7:37-38

REFLECTION

HOW WERE YOU IN AWE OF GOD THIS WEEK?

FREE SPACE

HABITS & RITUALS

PRAYER LIST

S M T W T F S

S M T W T F S

S M T W T F S

S M T W T F S

S M T W T F S

<table>
<tr><td>MAY</td><td>SUNDAY
23</td><td>MONDAY
24</td><td>TUESDAY
25</td></tr>
<tr><td>PRIORITIES</td><td>Pentecost Sunday</td><td>Victoria Day (CA)</td><td>MORNING</td></tr>
<tr><td></td><td>DAY</td><td>DAY</td><td>DAY</td></tr>
<tr><td></td><td>NIGHT</td><td>NIGHT</td><td>NIGHT</td></tr>
</table>

NOTES

<table>
<tr><th>WEDNESDAY 26</th><th>THURSDAY 27</th><th>FRIDAY 28</th><th>SATURDAY 29</th></tr>
<tr><td>MORNING</td><td>MORNING</td><td>MORNING</td><td>MORNING</td></tr>
<tr><td>DAY</td><td>DAY</td><td>DAY</td><td>DAY</td></tr>
<tr><td>NIGHT</td><td>NIGHT</td><td>NIGHT</td><td>NIGHT</td></tr>
</table>

TO DO LIST

<table>
<tr><th>JUNE</th><th>SUNDAY</th><th>MONDAY</th><th>TUESDAY</th></tr>
<tr><td>NOTES</td><td></td><td></td><td>1

Saint Justin</td></tr>
<tr><td></td><td>6   The Most Holy Body and Blood of Christ</td><td>7</td><td>8</td></tr>
<tr><td></td><td>13   Eleventh Sunday in Ordinary Time</td><td>14   Flag Day</td><td>15</td></tr>
<tr><td></td><td>20   Twelfth Sunday in Ordinary Time

Father's Day</td><td>21

Saint Aloysius Gonzaga</td><td>22

Saint Paulinus of Nola
Saints John Fisher & Thomas More</td></tr>
<tr><td></td><td>27   Thirteenth Sunday in Ordinary Time</td><td>28

Saint Irenaeus</td><td>29

Saints Peter & Paul</td></tr>
</table>

SAINT JUSTIN

- Feast Day: June 1
- Born: 100; Died: 165
- Patron saint of philosophers
- He was an early Christian apologist, who defended the Christian religion in writing.
- He studied many different schools of philosophy, but was left unsatisfied.
- He encountered an old man who convinced him that the testimony of the prophets were more reliable than the reasoning of philosophers.
- Most of his works are lost, but two apologies and a dialogue did survive.
- He was martyred alongside some of his students.

WEDNESDAY	THURSDAY	FRIDAY	SATURDAY
2 Saints Marcellinus & Peter	**3** Saint Charles Lwanga & Companions	**4**	**5** Saint Boniface
9 Saint Ephrem	**10**	**11** The Most Sacred Heart of Jesus Saint Barnabas	**12** The Immaculate Heart of the Blessed Virgin Mary
16	**17**	**18**	**19** Saint Romuald
23	**24** The Nativity of Saint John the Baptist	**25**	**26**
30 The First Martyrs of the Holy Roman Church			

GOALS

READING 1	READING 2	GOSPEL
Dt 4:32-34, 39-40	Romans 8:14-17	Matthew 28:16-20

Then Jesus approached and said to them, "All power in heaven and on earth has been given to me. Go, therefore and make disciples of all nations, baptizing them in the name of the Father, and of the Son, and of the holy Spirit, teaching them to observe all that I have commanded you. And behold, I am with you always, until the end of the age."

Matthew 28:18-20

REFLECTION

HOW WERE YOU IN AWE OF GOD THIS WEEK?

FREE SPACE

HABITS & RITUALS

| PRAYER LIST |

| S | M | T | W | T | F | S |

| S | M | T | W | T | F | S |

| S | M | T | W | T | F | S |

| S | M | T | W | T | F | S |

| S | M | T | W | T | F | S |

| | SUNDAY | MONDAY | TUESDAY |

PRIORITIES

30 SUNDAY
The Most Holy Trinity

31 MONDAY
Memorial Day

1 TUESDAY
MORNING

DAY

DAY

DAY

NIGHT

NIGHT

NIGHT

NOTES

| READING 1 | READING 2 | GOSPEL |

Exodus 24:3-8   Hebrews 9:11-15   Mark 14:12-16, 22-26

He said to them, "This is my blood of the covenant, which will be shed for many. Amen, I say to you, I shall not drink again the fruit of the vine until the day when I drink it new in the kingdom of God."

Mark 14:24-25

REFLECTION

HOW WERE YOU IN AWE OF GOD THIS WEEK?

WEEKLY RETREAT

FREE SPACE

HABITS & RITUALS

PRAYER LIST

S M T W T F S
S M T W T F S
S M T W T F S
S M T W T F S
S M T W T F S

<table>
<tr><td>JUNE</td><td>SUNDAY</td><td>MONDAY</td><td>TUESDAY</td></tr>
<tr><td>PRIORITIES</td><td>6
The Most Holy Body and Blood of Christ</td><td>7
MORNING</td><td>8
MORNING</td></tr>
<tr><td></td><td>DAY</td><td>DAY</td><td>DAY</td></tr>
<tr><td></td><td>NIGHT</td><td>NIGHT</td><td>NIGHT</td></tr>
</table>

NOTES

<table>
<tr><th>WEDNESDAY
9</th><th>THURSDAY
10</th><th>FRIDAY
11</th><th>SATURDAY
12</th></tr>
<tr><td>MORNING</td><td>MORNING</td><td>The Most Sacred Heart of Jesus</td><td>MORNING</td></tr>
<tr><td>DAY</td><td>DAY</td><td>DAY</td><td>DAY</td></tr>
<tr><td>NIGHT</td><td>NIGHT</td><td>NIGHT</td><td>NIGHT</td></tr>
</table>

TO DO

LIST

READING 1	READING 2	GOSPEL
Exodus 24:3-8	Hebrews 9:11-15	Mark 4:26-34

He said, "This is how it is with the kingdom of God; it is as if a man were to scatter seed on the land and would sleep and rise night and day and the seed would sprout and grow, he knows not how.

Mark 4:26-27

REFLECTION

HOW WERE YOU IN AWE OF GOD THIS WEEK?

FREE SPACE

HABITS & RITUALS

PRAYER LIST

S M T W T F S

S M T W T F S

S M T W T F S

S M T W T F S

S M T W T F S

<table>
<tr><td>JUNE</td><td>SUNDAY
13</td><td>MONDAY
14</td><td>TUESDAY
15</td></tr>
</table>

PRIORITIES

	SUNDAY 13	MONDAY 14	TUESDAY 15
MORNING		*Flag Day*	MORNING
DAY	DAY	DAY	DAY
NIGHT	NIGHT	NIGHT	NIGHT

NOTES

<table>
<tr><th>WEDNESDAY
16</th><th>THURSDAY
17</th><th>FRIDAY
18</th><th>SATURDAY
19</th></tr>
<tr><td>MORNING</td><td>MORNING</td><td>MORNING</td><td>MORNING</td></tr>
<tr><td>DAY</td><td>DAY</td><td>DAY</td><td>DAY</td></tr>
<tr><td>NIGHT</td><td>NIGHT</td><td>NIGHT</td><td>NIGHT</td></tr>
</table>

TO DO

LIST

READING 1	READING 2	GOSPEL
Job 38:1, 8-11	2 Corinthians 5:14-17	Mark 4:35-41

Jesus was in the stern, asleep on a cushion. They woke him and said to him, "Teacher, do you not care that we are perishing?" He woke up, rebuked the wind, and said to the sea, "Quiet! Be still!" The wind ceased and there was great calm. Then he asked them, "Why are you terrified? Do you not yet have faith?"

Mark 4:38-40

REFLECTION

HOW WERE YOU IN AWE OF GOD THIS WEEK?

FREE SPACE

HABITS & RITUALS

S M T W T F S

S M T W T F S

S M T W T F S

S M T W T F S

S M T W T F S

PRAYER LIST

<table>
<tr><td>JUNE</td><td>SUNDAY 20</td><td>MONDAY 21</td><td>TUESDAY 22</td></tr>
</table>

PRIORITIES

	SUNDAY 20	MONDAY 21	TUESDAY 22
	Father's Day	MORNING	MORNING
	DAY	DAY	DAY
	NIGHT	NIGHT	NIGHT

NOTES

<table>
<tr><td>WEDNESDAY
23</td><td>THURSDAY
24</td><td>FRIDAY
25</td><td>SATURDAY
26</td></tr>
<tr><td>MORNING</td><td>The Nativity of Saint John the Baptist</td><td>MORNING</td><td>MORNING</td></tr>
<tr><td>DAY</td><td>DAY</td><td>DAY</td><td>DAY</td></tr>
<tr><td>NIGHT</td><td>NIGHT</td><td>NIGHT</td><td>NIGHT</td></tr>
</table>

TO DO

LIST

<table>
<tr><td>JULY</td><td>SUNDAY</td><td>MONDAY</td><td>TUESDAY</td></tr>
<tr><td>NOTES</td><td></td><td></td><td></td></tr>
<tr><td></td><td>4 Fourteenth Sunday in Ordinary Time

Independence Day</td><td>5

Saint Anthony Zaccaria</td><td>6

Saint Maria Goretti</td></tr>
<tr><td></td><td>11 Fifteenth Sunday in Ordinary Time</td><td>12</td><td>13

Saint Henry</td></tr>
<tr><td></td><td>18 Sixteenth Sunday in Ordinary Time</td><td>19</td><td>20

Saint Apollinaris</td></tr>
<tr><td></td><td>25 Seventeenth Sunday in Ordinary Time</td><td>26

Saints Joachim & Anne</td><td>27</td></tr>
</table>

SAINT MARIA GORETTI

- Feast Day: July 6
- Born: October 16, 1890; Died: July 6, 1902
- Patron saint of victims of rape, crime victims, teenage girls, and modern youth
- She was born into a farming family.
- When her dad died when she was 9, she took over household duties.
- An 18 year old neighbor tried to make sexual advances and lead her into sin.
- She refused the man and he stabbed her.
- She forgave her murderer before her death two days later.
- The man converted to Christianity in prison after a dream of Maria handing him lilies.

<table>
<tr><th>WEDNESDAY</th><th>THURSDAY</th><th>FRIDAY</th><th>SATURDAY</th></tr>
<tr>
<td></td>
<td>1 Canada Day (CA)

Saint Junípero Serra</td>
<td>2</td>
<td>3

Saint Thomas</td>
</tr>
<tr>
<td>7</td>
<td>8</td>
<td>9

Saint Augustine Zhao Rong & Companions</td>
<td>10</td>
</tr>
<tr>
<td>14

Saint Kateri Tekakwitha</td>
<td>15

Saint Bonaventure</td>
<td>16 Our Lady of Mount Carmel</td>
<td>17</td>
</tr>
<tr>
<td>21

Saint Lawrence of Brindisi</td>
<td>22

Saint Mary Magdalene</td>
<td>23

Saint Bridget</td>
<td>24

Saint Sharbel Makhlūf</td>
</tr>
<tr>
<td>28</td>
<td>29

Saint Martha</td>
<td>30

Saint Peter Chrysologus</td>
<td>31

Saint Ignatius of Loyola</td>
</tr>
</table>

GOALS

| READING 1 | READING 2 | GOSPEL |

Wisdom 1:13-15, 2:23-24   2 Corinthians 8:7, 9, 13-15   Mark 5:21-43

One of the synagogue officials, named Jairus, came forward. Seeing him he fell at his feet and pleaded earnestly with him, saying, "My daughter is at the point of death. Please, come lay your hands on her that she may get well and live."

Mark 5:22-23

REFLECTION

HOW WERE YOU IN AWE OF GOD THIS WEEK?

FREE SPACE

HABITS & RITUALS

PRAYER LIST

| S | M | T | W | T | F | S |

| S | M | T | W | T | F | S |

| S | M | T | W | T | F | S |

| S | M | T | W | T | F | S |

| S | M | T | W | T | F | S |

	SUNDAY 27	MONDAY 28	TUESDAY 29
PRIORITIES	MORNING	MORNING	Saints Peter and Paul
	DAY	DAY	DAY
	NIGHT	NIGHT	NIGHT

NOTES

<table>
<tr><th>WEDNESDAY
30</th><th>THURSDAY
1</th><th>FRIDAY
2</th><th>SATURDAY
3</th></tr>
<tr><td>MORNING</td><td>*Canada Day (CA)*</td><td>MORNING</td><td>MORNING</td></tr>
<tr><td>DAY</td><td>DAY</td><td>DAY</td><td>DAY</td></tr>
<tr><td>NIGHT</td><td>NIGHT</td><td>NIGHT</td><td>NIGHT</td></tr>
</table>

TO DO

LIST

READING 1	READING 2	GOSPEL
Ezekiel 2:2-5	2 Corinthians 12:7-10	Mark 6:1-6a

Is he not the carpenter, the son of Mary, and the brother of James and Joses and Judas and Simon? And are not his sisters here with us?" And they took offense at him. Jesus said to them, "A prophet is not without honor except in his native place and among his own kin and in his own house."

Mark 6:3-4

REFLECTION

HOW WERE YOU IN AWE OF GOD THIS WEEK?

FREE SPACE

HABITS & RITUALS

| S | M | T | W | T | F | S |

PRAYER LIST

<table>
<tr><td>JULY</td><td>SUNDAY 4</td><td>MONDAY 5</td><td>TUESDAY 6</td></tr>
<tr><td>PRIORITIES</td><td>*Independence Day*</td><td>MORNING</td><td>MORNING</td></tr>
<tr><td></td><td>DAY</td><td>DAY</td><td>DAY</td></tr>
<tr><td></td><td>NIGHT</td><td>NIGHT</td><td>NIGHT</td></tr>
</table>

NOTES

<table>
<tr><td>WEDNESDAY 7</td><td>THURSDAY 8</td><td>FRIDAY 9</td><td>SATURDAY 10</td></tr>
<tr><td>MORNING</td><td>MORNING</td><td>MORNING</td><td>MORNING</td></tr>
<tr><td>DAY</td><td>DAY</td><td>DAY</td><td>DAY</td></tr>
<tr><td>NIGHT</td><td>NIGHT</td><td>NIGHT</td><td>NIGHT</td></tr>
</table>

TO DO

LIST

READING 1	READING 2	GOSPEL
Amos 7:12-15	Ephesians 1:3-14	Mark 6:7-13

He said to them, "Wherever you enter a house, stay there until you leave from there. Whatever place does not welcome you or listen to you, leave there and shake the dust off your feet in testimony against them." So they went off and preached repentance.

Mark 6:10-12

REFLECTION

HOW WERE YOU IN AWE OF GOD THIS WEEK?

FREE SPACE

HABITS & RITUALS

PRAYER LIST

S	M	T	W	T	F	S

S	M	T	W	T	F	S

S	M	T	W	T	F	S

S	M	T	W	T	F	S

S	M	T	W	T	F	S

<table>
<tr><td>JULY</td><td>SUNDAY
11</td><td>MONDAY
12</td><td>TUESDAY
13</td></tr>
<tr><td>PRIORITIES</td><td>MORNING</td><td>MORNING</td><td>MORNING</td></tr>
<tr><td></td><td>DAY</td><td>DAY</td><td>DAY</td></tr>
<tr><td></td><td>NIGHT</td><td>NIGHT</td><td>NIGHT</td></tr>
</table>

NOTES

<table>
<tr><th>WEDNESDAY 14</th><th>THURSDAY 15</th><th>FRIDAY 16</th><th>SATURDAY 17</th></tr>
<tr><td>MORNING</td><td>MORNING</td><td>MORNING</td><td>MORNING</td></tr>
<tr><td>DAY</td><td>DAY</td><td>DAY</td><td>DAY</td></tr>
<tr><td>NIGHT</td><td>NIGHT</td><td>NIGHT</td><td>NIGHT</td></tr>
</table>

TO DO

LIST

READING 1	READING 2	GOSPEL
Jeremiah 23:1-6	Ephesians 2:13-18	Mark 6:30-34

When he disembarked and saw the vast crowd, his heart was moved with pity for them, for they were like sheep without a shepherd; and he began to teach them many things.

Mark 6:34

REFLECTION

HOW WERE YOU IN AWE OF GOD THIS WEEK?

FREE SPACE

HABITS & RITUALS

PRAYER LIST

| S | M | T | W | T | F | S |

| S | M | T | W | T | F | S |

| S | M | T | W | T | F | S |

| S | M | T | W | T | F | S |

| S | M | T | W | T | F | S |

<table>
<tr><td>JULY</td><td>SUNDAY 18</td><td>MONDAY 19</td><td>TUESDAY 20</td></tr>
<tr><td>PRIORITIES</td><td>MORNING</td><td>MORNING</td><td>MORNING</td></tr>
<tr><td></td><td>DAY</td><td>DAY</td><td>DAY</td></tr>
<tr><td></td><td>NIGHT</td><td>NIGHT</td><td>NIGHT</td></tr>
</table>

NOTES

<table>
<tr><td>WEDNESDAY
21</td><td>THURSDAY
22</td><td>FRIDAY
23</td><td>SATURDAY
24</td></tr>
<tr><td>MORNING</td><td>MORNING</td><td>MORNING</td><td>MORNING</td></tr>
<tr><td>DAY</td><td>DAY</td><td>DAY</td><td>DAY</td></tr>
<tr><td>NIGHT</td><td>NIGHT</td><td>NIGHT</td><td>NIGHT</td></tr>
</table>

TO DO

LIST

READING 1	READING 2	GOSPEL
2 Kings 4:42-44	Ephesians 4:1-6	John 6:1-15

When Jesus raised his eyes and saw that a large crowd was coming to him, he said to Philip, "Where can we buy enough food for them to eat?" He said this to test him, because he himself knew what he was going to do. Philip answered him, "Two hundred days' wages worth of food would not be enough for each of them to have a little [bit]."

John 6:5-7

REFLECTION

HOW WERE YOU IN AWE OF GOD THIS WEEK?

FREE SPACE

HABITS & RITUALS

PRAYER LIST

S M T W T F S

S M T W T F S

S M T W T F S

S M T W T F S

S M T W T F S

<table>
<tr><td>JULY</td><td>SUNDAY 25</td><td>MONDAY 26</td><td>TUESDAY 27</td></tr>
</table>

PRIORITIES

	SUNDAY 25	MONDAY 26	TUESDAY 27
MORNING			
DAY			
NIGHT			

NOTES

<table>
<tr><th>WEDNESDAY 28</th><th>THURSDAY 29</th><th>FRIDAY 30</th><th>SATURDAY 31</th></tr>
<tr><td>MORNING</td><td>MORNING</td><td>MORNING</td><td>MORNING</td></tr>
<tr><td>DAY</td><td>DAY</td><td>DAY</td><td>DAY</td></tr>
<tr><td>NIGHT</td><td>NIGHT</td><td>NIGHT</td><td>NIGHT</td></tr>
</table>

TO DO LIST

<table>
<tr><th>AUGUST</th><th>SUNDAY</th><th>MONDAY</th><th>TUESDAY</th></tr>
<tr>
<td>NOTES</td>
<td>1
Eighteenth Sunday in Ordinary Time</td>
<td>2
Civic Holiday (CA)

Saint Eusebius of Vercelli
Saint Peter Julian Eymard</td>
<td>3</td>
</tr>
<tr>
<td></td>
<td>8
Ninteenth Sunday in Ordinary Time</td>
<td>9

Saint Teresa Benedicta of the Cross</td>
<td>10

Saint Lawrence</td>
</tr>
<tr>
<td></td>
<td>15
The Assumption of the Blessed Virigin Mary</td>
<td>16

Saint Stephen of Hungary</td>
<td>17</td>
</tr>
<tr>
<td></td>
<td>22
Twenty-First Sunday in Ordinary Time</td>
<td>23

Saint Rose of Lima</td>
<td>24

Saint Bartholomew</td>
</tr>
<tr>
<td></td>
<td>29
Twenty-Second Sunday in Ordinary Time</td>
<td>30</td>
<td>31</td>
</tr>
</table>

SAINT GENESIUS

- Feast Day: August 25
- Died: c. 303
- Patron saint of actors, comedians, and dancers
- He was a leader of a theatrical troupe and performed satirical plays that mocked Christianity.
- He performed in a play mocking baptism with Emperor Diocletian in the audience.
- When he was baptised in the play, he felt a weight on his chest.
- What he felt was the grace of God upon him and he affirmed his new Christian faith in front of the whole audience.
- Diocletian had him arrested, tortured, and later beheaded.

<table>
<tr><th>WEDNESDAY</th><th>THURSDAY</th><th>FRIDAY</th><th>SATURDAY</th></tr>
<tr>
<td>4

Saint John Vianney</td>
<td>5 The Dedication of the Basilica of Saint Mary Major

</td>
<td>6 The Transfiguration of the Lord

</td>
<td>7

Saint Sixtus II & Companions
Saint Cajetan</td>
</tr>
<tr>
<td>11

Saint Clare</td>
<td>12

Saint Jane Frances de Chantal</td>
<td>13

Saint Pontian & Hippolytus</td>
<td>14

Saint Maximilian Kolbe</td>
</tr>
<tr>
<td>18

</td>
<td>19

Saint John Eudes</td>
<td>20

Saint Bernard</td>
<td>21

Saint Pius X</td>
</tr>
<tr>
<td>25

Saint Louis
Saint Joseph Calasanz</td>
<td>26

</td>
<td>27

Saint Monica</td>
<td>28

Saint Augustine</td>
</tr>
<tr>
<td></td>
<td></td>
<td></td>
<td></td>
</tr>
</table>

GOALS

READING 1	READING 2	GOSPEL
Exodus 16:2-4, 12-15	Ephesians 4:17,20-24	John 6:24-35

Do not work for food that perishes but for the food that endures for eternal life, which the Son of Man will give you. For on him the Father, God, has set his seal." So they said to him, "What can we do to accomplish the works of God?" Jesus answered and said to them, "This is the work of God, that you believe in the one he sent."

John 6:27-29

REFLECTION

HOW WERE YOU IN AWE OF GOD THIS WEEK?

FREE SPACE

HABITS & RITUALS

S M T W T F S

S M T W T F S

S M T W T F S

S M T W T F S

S M T W T F S

PRAYER LIST

SUNDAY	MONDAY	TUESDAY
1	**2**	**3**

PRIORITIES

SUNDAY 1
MORNING

DAY

NIGHT

MONDAY 2
Civic Hoiday (CA)

DAY

NIGHT

TUESDAY 3
MORNING

DAY

NIGHT

NOTES

WEDNESDAY
4
THURSDAY
5
FRIDAY
6
SATURDAY
7
MORNING
MORNING
MORNING
MORNING
DAY
DAY
DAY
DAY
NIGHT
NIGHT
NIGHT
NIGHT
TO DO
LIST

READING 1	READING 2	GOSPEL
1 Kings 19:4-8	Ephesians 4:30—5:2	John 6:41-51

I am the bread of life. Your ancestors ate the manna in the desert, but they died; this is the bread that comes down from heaven so that one may eat it and not die. I am the living bread that came down from heaven; whoever eats this bread will live forever; and the bread that I will give is my flesh for the life of the world."

John 6:48-51

REFLECTION

HOW WERE YOU IN AWE OF GOD THIS WEEK?

WEEKLY RETREAT

FREE SPACE

HABITS & RITUALS

PRAYER LIST

S M T W T F S
S M T W T F S
S M T W T F S
S M T W T F S
S M T W T F S

<table>
<tr><td>AUGUST</td><td>SUNDAY 8</td><td>MONDAY 9</td><td>TUESDAY 10</td></tr>
<tr><td>PRIORITIES</td><td>MORNING</td><td>MORNING</td><td>MORNING</td></tr>
<tr><td></td><td>DAY</td><td>DAY</td><td>DAY</td></tr>
<tr><td></td><td>NIGHT</td><td>NIGHT</td><td>NIGHT</td></tr>
</table>

NOTES

<table>
<tr><td>WEDNESDAY 11</td><td>THURSDAY 12</td><td>FRIDAY 13</td><td>SATURDAY 14</td></tr>
<tr><td>MORNING</td><td>MORNING</td><td>MORNING</td><td>MORNING</td></tr>
<tr><td>DAY</td><td>DAY</td><td>DAY</td><td>DAY</td></tr>
<tr><td>NIGHT</td><td>NIGHT</td><td>NIGHT</td><td>NIGHT</td></tr>
</table>

TO DO LIST

READING 1	READING 2	GOSPEL
1 Chr 15:3-4, 15-16; 16:1-2	1 Corinthians 15:54b-57	Luke 11:27-28

While he was speaking, a woman from the crowd called out and said to him, "Blessed is the womb that carried you and the breasts at which you nursed." He replied, "Rather, blessed are those who hear the word of God and observe it."

Luke 11:27-28

REFLECTION

HOW WERE YOU IN AWE OF GOD THIS WEEK?

FREE SPACE

HABITS & RITUALS

PRAYER LIST

| S | M | T | W | T | F | S |

| S | M | T | W | T | F | S |

| S | M | T | W | T | F | S |

| S | M | T | W | T | F | S |

| S | M | T | W | T | F | S |

<table>
<tr><td>AUGUST</td><td>SUNDAY 15</td><td>MONDAY 16</td><td>TUESDAY 17</td></tr>
<tr><td>PRIORITIES</td><td>The Assumption of the Blessed Virgin Mary</td><td>MORNING</td><td>MORNING</td></tr>
<tr><td></td><td>DAY</td><td>DAY</td><td>DAY</td></tr>
<tr><td></td><td>NIGHT</td><td>NIGHT</td><td>NIGHT</td></tr>
</table>

NOTES

<table>
<tr><td>WEDNESDAY 18</td><td>THURSDAY 19</td><td>FRIDAY 20</td><td>SATURDAY 21</td></tr>
<tr><td>MORNING</td><td>MORNING</td><td>MORNING</td><td>MORNING</td></tr>
<tr><td>DAY</td><td>DAY</td><td>DAY</td><td>DAY</td></tr>
<tr><td>NIGHT</td><td>NIGHT</td><td>NIGHT</td><td>NIGHT</td></tr>
</table>

TO DO   **LIST**

READING 1	READING 2	GOSPEL
Joshua 24:1-2a, 15-17, 18b	Ephesians 5:21-32	John 6:60-69

But there are some of you who do not believe." Jesus knew from the beginning the ones who would not believe and the one who would betray him. And he said, "For this reason I have told you that no one can come to me unless it is granted him by my Father."

John 6:64-65

REFLECTION

HOW WERE YOU IN AWE OF GOD THIS WEEK?

FREE SPACE

HABITS & RITUALS

PRAYER LIST

S M T W T F S

S M T W T F S

S M T W T F S

S M T W T F S

S M T W T F S

AUGUST	SUNDAY 22	MONDAY 23	TUESDAY 24
PRIORITIES	MORNING	MORNING	MORNING
	DAY	DAY	DAY
	NIGHT	NIGHT	NIGHT

NOTES

<table>
<tr><th>WEDNESDAY 25</th><th>THURSDAY 26</th><th>FRIDAY 27</th><th>SATURDAY 28</th></tr>
<tr><td>MORNING</td><td>MORNING</td><td>MORNING</td><td>MORNING</td></tr>
<tr><td>DAY</td><td>DAY</td><td>DAY</td><td>DAY</td></tr>
<tr><td>NIGHT</td><td>NIGHT</td><td>NIGHT</td><td>NIGHT</td></tr>
</table>

TO DO LIST

NOTES

	SUNDAY	MONDAY	TUESDAY
5 Twenty-Third Sunday in Ordinary Time	**6** *Labor Day* / *Labour Day (CA)*	**7**
12 Twenty-Fourth Sunday in Ordinary Time	**13** Saint John Chrysostom	**14** The Exaltation of the Holy Cross
19 Twenty-Fifth Sunday in Ordinary Time	**20** Saints Andrew Kim Tae-gŏn & Paul Chŏng Ha-sang & Companions	**21** Saint Matthew
26 Twenty-Sixth Sunday in Ordinary Time	**27** Saint Vincent de Paul	**28** Saint Wenceslaus / Saint Lawrence Ruiz & Companions

SAINT JOSEPH OF CUPERTINO

- Feast Day: September 18
- Born: June 17, 1603; Died: September 18, 1663
- Patron saint of aviators and astronauts
- Joseph began to experience ecstatic visions as a child, which continued throughout his life.
- His ecstasies made him unfit for duties as a lay brother of the Capuchin friars, so he was dismissed.
- He worked in the stables of the Conventual friars and after several years was admitted to their Order and later ordained a priest.
- His ecstasies began to multiply and he levitated during the Mass for the Divine Office.
- He was deemed disruptive by his superiors and eventually confined to a small cell.

<table>
<tr><th>WEDNESDAY</th><th>THURSDAY</th><th>FRIDAY</th><th>SATURDAY</th></tr>
<tr><td>1</td><td>2</td><td>3

Saint Gregory the Great</td><td>4</td></tr>
<tr><td>8
The Nativity of the Blessed Virgin Mary</td><td>9

Saint Peter Claver</td><td>10</td><td>11</td></tr>
<tr><td>15
Our Lady of Sorrows</td><td>16

Saints Cornelius & Cyprian</td><td>17

Saint Robert Bellarmine</td><td>18

Saint Joseph of Cupertino</td></tr>
<tr><td>22</td><td>23

Saint Pius of Pietrelcina</td><td>24</td><td>25</td></tr>
<tr><td>29

Saints Michael, Gabriel, & Raphael</td><td>30

Saint Jerome</td><td></td><td></td></tr>
</table>

GOALS

READING 1	READING 2	GOSPEL

Deuteronomy 4:1-2, 6-8   James 1:17-18, 21b-22, 27   Mark 7:1-8, 14-15, 21-23

He summoned the crowd again and said to them, "Hear me, all of you, and understand. Nothing that enters one from outside can defile that person; but the things that come out from within are what defile."

Mark 7:14-15

REFLECTION

HOW WERE YOU IN AWE OF GOD THIS WEEK?

FREE SPACE

HABITS & RITUALS

S M T W T F S

S M T W T F S

S M T W T F S

S M T W T F S

S M T W T F S

PRAYER LIST

SUNDAY	MONDAY	TUESDAY
29	30	31

PRIORITIES

29 — SUNDAY

MORNING

DAY

NIGHT

30 — MONDAY

MORNING

DAY

NIGHT

31 — TUESDAY

MORNING

DAY

NIGHT

NOTES

<table>
<tr><th>WEDNESDAY 1</th><th>THURSDAY 2</th><th>FRIDAY 3</th><th>SATURDAY 4</th></tr>
<tr><td>MORNING</td><td>MORNING</td><td>MORNING</td><td>MORNING</td></tr>
<tr><td>DAY</td><td>DAY</td><td>DAY</td><td>DAY</td></tr>
<tr><td>NIGHT</td><td>NIGHT</td><td>NIGHT</td><td>NIGHT</td></tr>
</table>

TO DO LIST

READING 1	READING 2	GOSPEL
Isaiah 35:4-7a	James 2:1-5	Mark 7:31-37

He took him off by himself away from the crowd. He put his finger into the man's ears and, spitting, touched his tongue; then he looked up to heaven and groaned, and said to him, "Ephphatha!" (that is, "Be opened!")

Mark 7:33-34

REFLECTION

HOW WERE YOU IN AWE OF GOD THIS WEEK?

WEEKLY RETREAT

FREE SPACE

HABITS & RITUALS

PRAYER LIST

S M T W T F S

S M T W T F S

S M T W T F S

S M T W T F S

S M T W T F S

<table>
<tr><td>SEPTEMBER</td><td>SUNDAY
5</td><td>MONDAY
6</td><td>TUESDAY
7</td></tr>
<tr><td>PRIORITIES</td><td>MORNING</td><td>Labor Day
Labour Day (CA)</td><td>MORNING</td></tr>
<tr><td></td><td>DAY</td><td>DAY</td><td>DAY</td></tr>
<tr><td></td><td>NIGHT</td><td>NIGHT</td><td>NIGHT</td></tr>
</table>

NOTES

<table>
<tr><th>WEDNESDAY 8</th><th>THURSDAY 9</th><th>FRIDAY 10</th><th>SATURDAY 11</th></tr>
<tr><td>MORNING</td><td>MORNING</td><td>MORNING</td><td>MORNING</td></tr>
<tr><td>DAY</td><td>DAY</td><td>DAY</td><td>DAY</td></tr>
<tr><td>NIGHT</td><td>NIGHT</td><td>NIGHT</td><td>NIGHT</td></tr>
</table>

TO DO LIST

READING 1	READING 2	GOSPEL
Isaiah 50:4c-9a	James 2:14-18	Mark 8:27-35

He spoke this openly. Then Peter took him aside and began to rebuke him. At this he turned around and, looking at his disciples, rebuked Peter and said, "Get behind me, Satan. You are thinking not as God does, but as human beings do."

Mark 8:32-33

REFLECTION

HOW WERE YOU IN AWE OF GOD THIS WEEK?

FREE SPACE

HABITS & RITUALS

S	M	T	W	T	F	S

S	M	T	W	T	F	S

S	M	T	W	T	F	S

S	M	T	W	T	F	S

S	M	T	W	T	F	S

PRAYER LIST

	SUNDAY 12	MONDAY 13	TUESDAY 14

PRIORITIES

MORNING

MORNING

MORNING

DAY

DAY

DAY

NIGHT

NIGHT

NIGHT

NOTES

<table>
<tr><th>WEDNESDAY
15</th><th>THURSDAY
16</th><th>FRIDAY
17</th><th>SATURDAY
18</th></tr>
<tr><td>MORNING</td><td>MORNING</td><td>MORNING</td><td>MORNING</td></tr>
<tr><td>DAY</td><td>DAY</td><td>DAY</td><td>DAY</td></tr>
<tr><td>NIGHT</td><td>NIGHT</td><td>NIGHT</td><td>NIGHT</td></tr>
</table>

TO DO

LIST

READING 1	READING 2	GOSPEL
Wisdom 2:12, 17-20	James 3:16—4:3	Mark 9:30-37

But they remained silent. They had been discussing among themselves on the way who was the greatest. Then he sat down, called the Twelve, and said to them, "If anyone wishes to be first, he shall be the last of all and the servant of all."

Mark 9:34-35

REFLECTION

HOW WERE YOU IN AWE OF GOD THIS WEEK?

WEEKLY RETREAT

FREE SPACE

HABITS & RITUALS

PRAYER LIST

S M T W T F S
S M T W T F S
S M T W T F S
S M T W T F S
S M T W T F S

SEPTEMBER

PRIORITIES

SUNDAY 19
MONDAY 20
TUESDAY 21

MORNING

DAY

NIGHT

NOTES

<table>
<tr><th>WEDNESDAY 22</th><th>THURSDAY 23</th><th>FRIDAY 24</th><th>SATURDAY 25</th></tr>
<tr><td>MORNING</td><td>MORNING</td><td>MORNING</td><td>MORNING</td></tr>
<tr><td>DAY</td><td>DAY</td><td>DAY</td><td>DAY</td></tr>
<tr><td>NIGHT</td><td>NIGHT</td><td>NIGHT</td><td>NIGHT</td></tr>
</table>

TO DO

LIST

<table>
<tr><th>OCTOBER</th><th>SUNDAY</th><th>MONDAY</th><th>TUESDAY</th></tr>
<tr><td>NOTES</td><td></td><td></td><td></td></tr>
<tr><td></td><td>3   Twenty-Seventh Sunday in Ordinary Time</td><td>4

Saint Francis of Assisi</td><td>5

Blessed Francis Xavier Seelos</td></tr>
<tr><td></td><td>10   Twenty-Eighth Sunday in Ordinary Time

Saint Francis Borgia</td><td>11   *Columbus Day*
Indigenous Peoples' Day
Thanksgiving (CA)

Saint John XXIII</td><td>12</td></tr>
<tr><td></td><td>17   Twenty-Ninth Sunday in Ordinary Time</td><td>18

Saint Luke</td><td>19

Saints John de Brébeuf & Isaac Jogues & Companions</td></tr>
<tr><td></td><td>24   Thirtieth Sunday in Ordinary Time</td><td>25</td><td>26</td></tr>
<tr><td></td><td>31   Thirty-First Sunday in Ordinary Time</td><td></td><td></td></tr>
</table>

SAINT FRANCIS BORGIA

- Feast Day: October 10
- Born: October 28, 1510; Died: September 30, 1572
- Patron saint of Portugal; against earthquakes
- Francis was the 4th Duke of Gandía.
- When his wife died, he entered the newly formed Society of Jesus.
- He then renounced his titles and became a priest.

- He helped in the establishment of what is now the Gregorian University in Rome.
- He felt drawn to spend time in seclusion and prayer, so he fled to the Basque Country to avoid the Pope's intention to make him a cardinal.
- He later became the Jesuit commissary-general in Spain, where he founded a dozen colleges.

<table>
<tr><th>WEDNESDAY</th><th>THURSDAY</th><th>FRIDAY</th><th>SATURDAY</th></tr>
<tr><td></td><td></td><td>1

Saint Thérèse of the Child Jesus</td><td>2 The Holy Guardian Angels</td></tr>
<tr><td>6

Saint Bruno</td><td>7 Our Lady of the Rosary</td><td>8</td><td>9

Saint Denis
Saint John Leonardi</td></tr>
<tr><td>13</td><td>14

Saint Caliistus I</td><td>15

Saint Teresa of Jesus</td><td>16

Saint Hedwig
Saint Margaret Mary Alacoque</td></tr>
<tr><td>20

Saint Paul of the Cross</td><td>21</td><td>22

Saint John Paul II</td><td>23

Saint John Capistrano</td></tr>
<tr><td>27</td><td>28

Saints Simon & Jude</td><td>29</td><td>30</td></tr>
</table>

READING 1	READING 2	GOSPEL
Numbers 11:25-29	James 5:1-6	Mark 9:38-43, 45, 47-48

Jesus replied, "Do not prevent him. There is no one who performs a mighty deed in my name who can at the same time speak ill of me. For whoever is not against us is for us. Anyone who gives you a cup of water to drink because you belong to Christ, amen, I say to you, will surely not lose his reward.

Mark 9:39-41

REFLECTION

HOW WERE YOU IN AWE OF GOD THIS WEEK?

WEEKLY RETREAT

FREE SPACE

HABITS & RITUALS

PRAYER LIST

S M T W T F S

S M T W T F S

S M T W T F S

S M T W T F S

S M T W T F S

| SUNDAY 26 | MONDAY 27 | TUESDAY 28 |

PRIORITIES

MORNING	MORNING	MORNING
DAY	DAY	DAY
NIGHT	NIGHT	NIGHT

NOTES

<table>
<tr><th>WEDNESDAY 29</th><th>THURSDAY 30</th><th>FRIDAY 1</th><th>SATURDAY 2</th></tr>
<tr><td>MORNING</td><td>MORNING</td><td>MORNING</td><td>MORNING</td></tr>
<tr><td>DAY</td><td>DAY</td><td>DAY</td><td>DAY</td></tr>
<tr><td>NIGHT</td><td>NIGHT</td><td>NIGHT</td><td>NIGHT</td></tr>
</table>

TO DO

LIST

READING 1	READING 2	GOSPEL
Genesis 2:18-24	Hebrews 2:9-11	Mark 10:2-16

When Jesus saw this he became indignant and said to them, "Let the children come to me; do not prevent them, for the kingdom of God belongs to such as these. Amen, I say to you, whoever does not accept the kingdom of God like a child will not enter it."

Mark 10:14-15

REFLECTION

HOW WERE YOU IN AWE OF GOD THIS WEEK?

FREE SPACE

HABITS & RITUALS

S M T W T F S

S M T W T F S

S M T W T F S

S M T W T F S

S M T W T F S

PRAYER LIST

OCTOBER

PRIORITIES

SUNDAY
3
MONDAY
4
TUESDAY
5

MORNING
MORNING
MORNING

DAY
DAY
DAY

NIGHT
NIGHT
NIGHT

NOTES

<table>
<tr><th>WEDNESDAY
6</th><th>THURSDAY
7</th><th>FRIDAY
8</th><th>SATURDAY
9</th></tr>
<tr><td>MORNING</td><td>MORNING</td><td>MORNING</td><td>MORNING</td></tr>
<tr><td>DAY</td><td>DAY</td><td>DAY</td><td>DAY</td></tr>
<tr><td>NIGHT</td><td>NIGHT</td><td>NIGHT</td><td>NIGHT</td></tr>
</table>

TO DO LIST

READING 1	READING 2	GOSPEL
Wisdom 7:7-11	Hebrews 4:12-13	Mark 10:17-30

Jesus, looking at him, loved him and said to him, "You are lacking in one thing. Go, sell what you have, and give to [the] poor and you will have treasure in heaven; then come, follow me." At that statement his face fell, and he went away sad, for he had many possessions.

Mark 10:21-22

REFLECTION

HOW WERE YOU IN AWE OF GOD THIS WEEK?

FREE SPACE

HABITS & RITUALS

PRAYER LIST

S M T W T F S

S M T W T F S

S M T W T F S

S M T W T F S

S M T W T F S

PRIORITIES	SUNDAY 10	MONDAY 11	TUESDAY 12
	MORNING	*Columbus Day* *Indigenous Peoples' Day* *Thanksgiving (CA)*	MORNING
	DAY	DAY	DAY
	NIGHT	NIGHT	NIGHT

NOTES

WEDNESDAY 13	THURSDAY 14	FRIDAY 15	SATURDAY 16
MORNING	MORNING	MORNING	MORNING
DAY	DAY	DAY	DAY
NIGHT	NIGHT	NIGHT	NIGHT

TO DO LIST

READING 1	READING 2	GOSPEL
Isaiah 53:10-11	Hebrews 4:14-16	Mark 10:35-45

But it shall not be so among you. Rather, whoever wishes to be great among you will be your servant; whoever wishes to be first among you will be the slave of all. For the Son of Man did not come to be served but to serve and to give his life as a ransom for many."

Mark 10:43-45

REFLECTION

HOW WERE YOU IN AWE OF GOD THIS WEEK?

FREE SPACE

HABITS & RITUALS

PRAYER LIST

| S | M | T | W | T | F | S |

| S | M | T | W | T | F | S |

| S | M | T | W | T | F | S |

| S | M | T | W | T | F | S |

| S | M | T | W | T | F | S |

OCTOBER	SUNDAY 17	MONDAY 18	TUESDAY 19
PRIORITIES	MORNING	MORNING	MORNING
	DAY	DAY	DAY
	NIGHT	NIGHT	NIGHT

NOTES

WEDNESDAY 20	THURSDAY 21	FRIDAY 22	SATURDAY 23
MORNING	MORNING	MORNING	MORNING
DAY	DAY	DAY	DAY
NIGHT	NIGHT	NIGHT	NIGHT

TO DO LIST

READING 1	READING 2	GOSPEL
Jeremiah 31:7-9	Hebrews 5:1-6	Mark 10:46-52

Jesus said to him in reply, "What do you want me to do for you?" The blind man replied to him, "Master, I want to see." Jesus told him, "Go your way; your faith has saved you." Immediately he received his sight and followed him on the way.

Mark 10:51-52

REFLECTION

HOW WERE YOU IN AWE OF GOD THIS WEEK?

FREE SPACE

HABITS & RITUALS

| S | M | T | W | T | F | S |

| S | M | T | W | T | F | S |

| S | M | T | W | T | F | S |

| S | M | T | W | T | F | S |

| S | M | T | W | T | F | S |

PRAYER LIST

SUNDAY 24	MONDAY 25	TUESDAY 26

PRIORITIES

SUNDAY 24

MORNING

DAY

NIGHT

MONDAY 25

MORNING

DAY

NIGHT

TUESDAY 26

MORNING

DAY

NIGHT

NOTES

<table>
<tr><th>WEDNESDAY 27</th><th>THURSDAY 28</th><th>FRIDAY 29</th><th>SATURDAY 30</th></tr>
<tr><td>MORNING</td><td>MORNING</td><td>MORNING</td><td>MORNING</td></tr>
<tr><td>DAY</td><td>DAY</td><td>DAY</td><td>DAY</td></tr>
<tr><td>NIGHT</td><td>NIGHT</td><td>NIGHT</td><td>NIGHT</td></tr>
</table>

TO DO

LIST

NOTES

1 — All Saints

2 — All Souls' Day

7 — Thirty-Second Sunday in Ordinary Time
Daylight Saving Time End

8

9 — The Dedication of the Lateran Basilica

14 — Thirty-Third Sunday in Ordinary Time

15 — Saint Albert the Great

16 — Saint Margaret of Scotland / Saint Gertrude

21 — Our Lord Jesus Christ, King of the Universe

22 — Saint Cecilia

23 — Saint Clement I / Saint Columban / Blessed Miguel Agustín Pro

28 — First Sunday of Advent

29

30 — Saint Andrew

SAINT CATHERINE OF ALEXANDRIA

- Feast Day: November 25
- Born: c. 287; Died: c. 305
- Patron saint of unmarried girls, educators, nurses, librarians, and craftsmen who work with a wheel
- Emperor Maxentius summoned 50 pagan philosophers to debate with Catherine.
- Several philosophers converted after her win.
- Catherine was imprisoned and had many visitors, including Maxentius' wife, who converted.
- When she was released, a bright light and fragrant perfume filled the dungeon.
- She refused the emperor's marriage proposal.
- She was condemned to death on a spiked breaking wheel, but it shattered at her touch.

<table>
<tr><th>WEDNESDAY</th><th>THURSDAY</th><th>FRIDAY</th><th>SATURDAY</th></tr>
<tr>
<td>3

Saint Martin de Porres</td>
<td>4

Saint Charles Borromeo</td>
<td>5</td>
<td>6</td>
</tr>
<tr>
<td>10

Saint Leo the Great</td>
<td>11
Veterans Day
Remembrance Day (CA)

Saint Martin of Tours</td>
<td>12

Saint Josaphat</td>
<td>13

Saint Francis Xavier Cabrini</td>
</tr>
<tr>
<td>17

Saint Elizabeth of Hungary</td>
<td>18
The Dedication of the Basilicas of Saints Peter & Paul

Saint Rose Philippine Duschesne</td>
<td>19</td>
<td>20</td>
</tr>
<tr>
<td>24

Saint Andrew Dũng-Lạc</td>
<td>25
Thanksgiving

Saint Catherine of Alexandria</td>
<td>26</td>
<td>27</td>
</tr>
<tr>
<td></td>
<td></td>
<td></td>
<td></td>
</tr>
</table>

READING 1	READING 2	GOSPEL
Deuteronomy 6:2-6	Hebrews 7:23-28	Mark 12:28b-34

The scribe said to him, "Well said, teacher. You are right in saying, 'He is One and there is no other than he.' And 'to love him with all your heart, with all your understanding, with all your strength, and to love your neighbor as yourself' is worth more than all burnt offerings and sacrifices."

Mark 12:32-33

REFLECTION

HOW WERE YOU IN AWE OF GOD THIS WEEK?

FREE SPACE

HABITS & RITUALS

S	M	T	W	T	F	S

S	M	T	W	T	F	S

S	M	T	W	T	F	S

S	M	T	W	T	F	S

S	M	T	W	T	F	S

PRAYER LIST

31 / **1** / **2**

MORNING

All Saints

All Souls' Day

DAY | **DAY** | **DAY**

NIGHT | **NIGHT** | **NIGHT**

NOTES

WEDNESDAY
3
THURSDAY
4
FRIDAY
5
SATURDAY
6

MORNING
MORNING
MORNING
MORNING

DAY
DAY
DAY
DAY

NIGHT
NIGHT
NIGHT
NIGHT

TO DO
LIST

READING 1	READING 2	GOSPEL
1 Kings 17:10-16	Hebrews 9:24-28	Mark 12:38-44

In the course of his teaching he said, "Beware of the scribes, who like to go around in long robes and accept greetings in the marketplaces, seats of honor in synagogues, and places of honor at banquets.

Mark 12:38-39

REFLECTION

HOW WERE YOU IN AWE OF GOD THIS WEEK?

FREE SPACE

HABITS & RITUALS

PRAYER LIST

S M T W T F S

S M T W T F S

S M T W T F S

S M T W T F S

S M T W T F S

<table>
<tr><td>NOVEMBER</td><td>SUNDAY 7</td><td>MONDAY 8</td><td>TUESDAY 9</td></tr>
<tr><td>PRIORITIES</td><td>Daylight Saving Time End</td><td>MORNING</td><td>MORNING</td></tr>
<tr><td></td><td>DAY</td><td>DAY</td><td>DAY</td></tr>
<tr><td></td><td>NIGHT</td><td>NIGHT</td><td>NIGHT</td></tr>
</table>

NOTES

<table>
<tr><th>WEDNESDAY 10</th><th>THURSDAY 11</th><th>FRIDAY 12</th><th>SATURDAY 13</th></tr>
<tr><td>MORNING</td><td>Veterans Day
Remembrance Day (CA)</td><td>MORNING</td><td>MORNING</td></tr>
<tr><td>DAY</td><td>DAY</td><td>DAY</td><td>DAY</td></tr>
<tr><td>NIGHT</td><td>NIGHT</td><td>NIGHT</td><td>NIGHT</td></tr>
</table>

TO DO LIST

READING 1	READING 2	GOSPEL
Daniel 12:1-3	Hebrews 10:11-14, 18	Mark 13:24-32

"Learn a lesson from the fig tree. When its branch becomes tender and sprouts leaves, you know that summer is near. In the same way, when you see these things happening, know that he is near, at the gates.

Mark 13:28-29

REFLECTION

HOW WERE YOU IN AWE OF GOD THIS WEEK?

FREE SPACE

HABITS & RITUALS

PRAYER LIST

| S | M | T | W | T | F | S |

| S | M | T | W | T | F | S |

| S | M | T | W | T | F | S |

| S | M | T | W | T | F | S |

| S | M | T | W | T | F | S |

<table>
<tr><td>NOVEMBER</td><td>SUNDAY 14</td><td>MONDAY 15</td><td>TUESDAY 16</td></tr>
<tr><td>PRIORITIES</td><td>MORNING</td><td>MORNING</td><td>MORNING</td></tr>
<tr><td></td><td>DAY</td><td>DAY</td><td>DAY</td></tr>
<tr><td></td><td>NIGHT</td><td>NIGHT</td><td>NIGHT</td></tr>
</table>

NOTES

<table>
<tr><th>WEDNESDAY 17</th><th>THURSDAY 18</th><th>FRIDAY 19</th><th>SATURDAY 20</th></tr>
<tr><td>MORNING</td><td>MORNING</td><td>MORNING</td><td>MORNING</td></tr>
<tr><td>DAY</td><td>DAY</td><td>DAY</td><td>DAY</td></tr>
<tr><td>NIGHT</td><td>NIGHT</td><td>NIGHT</td><td>NIGHT</td></tr>
</table>

TO DO

LIST

READING 1	READING 2	GOSPEL
Daniel 7:13-14	Revelation 1:5-8	John 18:33b-37

So Pilate said to him, "Then you are a king?" Jesus answered, "You say I am a king. For this I was born and for this I came into the world, to testify to the truth. Everyone who belongs to the truth listens to my voice."

John 18:37

REFLECTION

HOW WERE YOU IN AWE OF GOD THIS WEEK?

FREE SPACE

HABITS & RITUALS

PRAYER LIST

S M T W T F S

S M T W T F S

S M T W T F S

S M T W T F S

S M T W T F S

<table>
<tr><td>NOVEMBER</td><td>SUNDAY
21</td><td>MONDAY
22</td><td>TUESDAY
23</td></tr>
<tr><td>PRIORITIES</td><td>Our Lord Jesus Christ,
King of the Universe</td><td>MORNING</td><td>MORNING</td></tr>
<tr><td></td><td>DAY</td><td>DAY</td><td>DAY</td></tr>
<tr><td></td><td>NIGHT</td><td>NIGHT</td><td>NIGHT</td></tr>
</table>

NOTES

<table>
<tr><td>WEDNESDAY
24</td><td>THURSDAY
25</td><td>FRIDAY
26</td><td>SATURDAY
27</td></tr>
<tr><td>MORNING</td><td>*Thanksgiving*</td><td>MORNING</td><td>MORNING</td></tr>
<tr><td>DAY</td><td>DAY</td><td>DAY</td><td>DAY</td></tr>
<tr><td>NIGHT</td><td>NIGHT</td><td>NIGHT</td><td>NIGHT</td></tr>
</table>

TO DO

LIST

NOTES

5 Second Sunday of Advent

6
Saint Nicholas

7
Saint Ambrose

12 Third Sunday of Advent

13
Saint Lucy

14
Saint John of the Cross

19 Fourth Sunday of Advent

20

21
Saint Peter Canisius

26 The Holy Family of Jesus, Mary and Joseph

Boxing Day (CA)

27
Saint John

28 The Holy Innocents

SAINT FRANCIS XAVIER

- Feast Day: December 3
- Born: April 7, 1506; Died: December 2, 1552
- Patron saint of missionaries and missions
- Saint Ignatius convinced Francis to become a priest while both attended the University of Paris.
- Francis, Ignatius, and other friends vowed to travel to the Holy Land to convert non-believers.
- Francis was appointed by Ignatius to help establish the Society of Jesus (the Jesuits) in Portugal. Thus, beginning his life as the first Jesuit missionary.
- Francis devoted much of his life to missions especially in Asia - mainly Malacca, Amboina and Ternate, Japan, and off-shore China.

WEDNESDAY	THURSDAY	FRIDAY	SATURDAY
1	2	3 Saint Francis Xavier	4 Saint John Damascene
8 The Immaculate Conception of the Blessed Virgin Mary	9 Saint Juan Diego	10 Our Lady of Loreto	11 Saint Damasus I
15	16	17	18
22	23 Saint John of Kanty	24	25 The Nativity of the Lord, Christimas
29 Saint Thomas Becket	30	31 Saint Sylvester I	

| READING 1 | READING 2 | GOSPEL |

Jeremiah 33:14-16   1 Thessalonians 3:12—4:2   Luke 21:25-28, 34-36

"Beware that your hearts do not become drowsy from carousing and drunkenness and the anxieties of daily life, and that day catch you by surprise like a trap. For that day will assault everyone who lives on the face of the earth.

Luke 21:34-35

REFLECTION

HOW WERE YOU IN AWE OF GOD THIS WEEK?

FREE SPACE

HABITS & RITUALS

PRAYER LIST

| S | M | T | W | T | F | S |

| S | M | T | W | T | F | S |

| S | M | T | W | T | F | S |

| S | M | T | W | T | F | S |

| S | M | T | W | T | F | S |

	SUNDAY	MONDAY	TUESDAY
PRIORITIES	28	29	30

SUNDAY 28

MORNING

DAY

NIGHT

MONDAY 29

MORNING

DAY

NIGHT

TUESDAY 30

MORNING

DAY

NIGHT

NOTES

READING 1	READING 2	GOSPEL
Baruch 5:1-9	Philippians 1:5-6, 8-11	Luke 3:1-6

Every valley shall be filled and every mountain and hill shall be made low. The winding roads shall be made straight, and the rough ways made smooth, and all flesh shall see the salvation of God.'"

Luke 3:5-6

REFLECTION

HOW WERE YOU IN AWE OF GOD THIS WEEK?

FREE SPACE

HABITS & RITUALS

| S | M | T | W | T | F | S |

| S | M | T | W | T | F | S |

| S | M | T | W | T | F | S |

| S | M | T | W | T | F | S |

| S | M | T | W | T | F | S |

PRAYER LIST

SUNDAY 5	MONDAY 6	TUESDAY 7
MORNING	MORNING	MORNING
DAY	DAY	DAY
NIGHT	NIGHT	NIGHT

PRIORITIES

NOTES

<table>
<tr><th>WEDNESDAY
8</th><th>THURSDAY
9</th><th>FRIDAY
10</th><th>SATURDAY
11</th></tr>
<tr><td>The Immaculate Conception
of the Blessed Virgin Mary</td><td>MORNING</td><td>MORNING</td><td>MORNING</td></tr>
<tr><td>DAY</td><td>DAY</td><td>DAY</td><td>DAY</td></tr>
<tr><td>NIGHT</td><td>NIGHT</td><td>NIGHT</td><td>NIGHT</td></tr>
</table>

TO DO

LIST

| READING 1 | READING 2 | GOSPEL |

Zephaniah 3:14-18a

Philippians 4:4-7

Luke 3:10-18

John answered them all, saying, "I am baptizing you with water, but one mightier than I is coming. I am not worthy to loosen the thongs of his sandals. He will baptize you with the holy Spirit and fire.

Luke 3:16

REFLECTION

HOW WERE YOU IN AWE OF GOD THIS WEEK?

FREE SPACE

HABITS & RITUALS

PRAYER LIST

S M T W T F S

S M T W T F S

S M T W T F S

S M T W T F S

S M T W T F S

DECEMBER

PRIORITIES

SUNDAY 12

MONDAY 13

TUESDAY 14

MORNING

MORNING

MORNING

DAY

DAY

DAY

NIGHT

NIGHT

NIGHT

NOTES

<table>
<tr><th>WEDNESDAY
15</th><th>THURSDAY
16</th><th>FRIDAY
17</th><th>SATURDAY
18</th></tr>
<tr><td>MORNING</td><td>MORNING</td><td>MORNING</td><td>MORNING</td></tr>
<tr><td>DAY</td><td>DAY</td><td>DAY</td><td>DAY</td></tr>
<tr><td>NIGHT</td><td>NIGHT</td><td>NIGHT</td><td>NIGHT</td></tr>
</table>

TO DO LIST

| READING 1 | READING 2 | GOSPEL |

Micah 5:1-4a   Hebrews 10:5-10   Luke 1:39-45

When Elizabeth heard Mary's greeting, the infant leaped in her womb, and Elizabeth, filled with the holy Spirit, cried out in a loud voice and said, "Most blessed are you among women, and blessed is the fruit of your womb.

Luke 1:41-42

REFLECTION

HOW WERE YOU IN AWE OF GOD THIS WEEK?

FREE SPACE

HABITS & RITUALS

PRAYER LIST

| S | M | T | W | T | F | S |

| S | M | T | W | T | F | S |

| S | M | T | W | T | F | S |

| S | M | T | W | T | F | S |

| S | M | T | W | T | F | S |

<table>
<tr><td>DECEMBER</td><td>SUNDAY 19</td><td>MONDAY 20</td><td>TUESDAY 21</td></tr>
</table>

PRIORITIES

	MORNING	MORNING	MORNING
	DAY	DAY	DAY
	NIGHT	NIGHT	NIGHT

NOTES

<table>
<tr><th>WEDNESDAY
22</th><th>THURSDAY
23</th><th>FRIDAY
24</th><th>SATURDAY
25</th></tr>
<tr><td>MORNING</td><td>MORNING</td><td>MORNING</td><td>**The Nativity of the Lord
Christmas**</td></tr>
<tr><td>DAY</td><td>DAY</td><td>DAY</td><td>DAY</td></tr>
<tr><td>NIGHT</td><td>NIGHT</td><td>NIGHT</td><td>NIGHT</td></tr>
</table>

TO DO LIST

READING 1	READING 2	GOSPEL
Sirach 3:2-6, 12-14	Colossians 3:12-21	Luke 2:41-52

When his parents saw him, they were astonished, and his mother said to him, "Son, why have you done this to us? Your father and I have been looking for you with great anxiety." And he said to them, "Why were you looking for me? Did you not know that I must be in my Father's house?"

Luke 2:48-49

REFLECTION

HOW WERE YOU IN AWE OF GOD THIS WEEK?

FREE SPACE

HABITS & RITUALS

| S | M | T | W | T | F | S |

| S | M | T | W | T | F | S |

| S | M | T | W | T | F | S |

| S | M | T | W | T | F | S |

| S | M | T | W | T | F | S |

PRAYER LIST

<table>
<tr><td>DEC & JAN</td><td>SUNDAY 26</td><td>MONDAY 27</td><td>TUESDAY 28</td></tr>
</table>

PRIORITIES

Boxing Day (CA)	MORNING	MORNING
DAY	DAY	DAY
NIGHT	NIGHT	NIGHT

NOTES

MORNING	MORNING	MORNING	*New Year's Day*
DAY	DAY	DAY	DAY
NIGHT	NIGHT	NIGHT	NIGHT

TO DO

LIST

Congratulations! You made it through 2021!
Look back at your Path to Sainthood and reflect on the year you accomplished.